This book is dedicated to my parents, James Nicol and Mary Fowler Nicol to whom I owed everything. The Nicol Family approximately 1918. Left to Right Jack, Dad, Eva, Jim, Myself and at the front Ernest.

Mum

P. L. Nicol
July, 1995

Front Cover "Girls Entrance" to Central School, 1906

LIKE TOPSY IT JUST GROWED AND GROWED

I started these notes on the old days just for fun, but just like "Topsy" they just growed and growed. Correspondence from "Bluemogganers" all over the world, made the work more than worthwhile.

Every now and then some other memory would come to me, sometimes while reading, sometimes while watching T.V. and sometimes in the dead of night, when I should have been asleep! Sometimes a "kent" face would open a door, sometimes an old photo, who knows? Memories are funny things, and if I sometimes get things wrong, well that's what memories are like!

My memory was jogged on several occasions by letters received from readers - letters like the one I received from H. L. Henderson, Musselburgh explaining the meaning of Sandikie Robertsons nickname "Shokio". Apparently this was originally Shokiay, which referred to a choker or collar which Mr. Robertson wore. In order to impress "Madame" the word was "Frenchified" and became "Shokiay". This was further extended to become Sherlock Shokiay when Mr. Robertson announced one day that he was doing a bit of detective work to discover who had apparently done some damage to equipment in the woodwork room.

Or one of several letters from Canada. This one was from Jack McKay in Ontario. Despite the fact that his limbs were so badly affected by nerve pressure that it was only with great difficulty that he could even hold a pen, Jack had laboriously printed this letter. Not knowing who the writer P.L.N. was he sent it to his sister in Peterhead asking her to try and identify the writer and pass it on. This she eventually succeeded in doing. He could scarcely believe that "Aik" White allowed children into his workshop, but I was able to assure him that it was true. Jack remembered vividly the Scout band with the brothers Mutt and Jeff Brown, and the wonderful camps at Blackhills. Another Canadian letter was even more interesting. It came from "Clyne Music Centre" Kelowna B.C. and was signed "Maple Leaf". This lady and her hubby were particularly interested in my article which referred to the tunnel under Broad Street. Apparently Mrs. Clyne was brought up in one of the lodges at Dales House, and she had been told so often about the tunnel which was supposed to go from Dales House to Arbuthnot House in Broad Street! She had even been shown a trap-door in a room there, which was the start of the tunnel! The tunnel was reputed to have been used by whisky smugglers! They were also very interested in my articles about Mr. Robertson, as they had been close friends of the Robertson family! They had enjoyed many happy music at evenings together both at St, Mary Street and Rora!

Another encouraging letter came from my old friend the late Tom Gibb, who I was delighted to see had been asked to address his old school Peterhead Academy a well deserved honour! Tom apparently found pleasure in being reminded of our childhood in the "Blue Toon", as did his sister with whom he lived in Aberdeen.

Another old classmate came up with some very interesting information. Alex Sutherland who was at the time a "postie" wrote to tell me that quite a few of our old class-mates were still living in Peterhead! Among them were Emanuel Evans, Sandie Scott (garage), Danny Maclean, Chrissie Mess, "Bet" Yule, Alex Wallace, Johnny Matthew, Alex Reid and Henry Relph. Alas several have now passed on! It really was a pleasure to receive those letters.

Peter Nicol and Alex Sutherland's Class 1921
Middle Row, 3rd from right Alex Sutherland, 5th from right Peter Nicol

"THE GOOD OLD DAYS?" IN THE "BLUE TOON"

By splashing stream or placid pool
'Neath Ugie's Pinkie Braes
It never rained on Ugie-side
In the good old days.

On the old coach road by plantins four
My childhood memory says
It never rained in the summer time
In the good old days.

By Babbie Duthie's rock and craig
'Mid Ugie's winding ways
It never rained at Ravenscraig
In the good old days.

On the golf course with its fairways keen
Scorched brown by the hot sun's rays
It never rained on Craigewan's links
In the good old days.

By the mineral well or the mountain
Along the Gadle Braes
It never rained by the sea shore
In the good old days.

Catching buddocks, geats or podlies
On the embankment - what a craze
It never rained at the fishing
In the good old days.

Up Johnnie Matha's roadie
Bird nesting by its ways
It never rained at Easter
In the good old days.

On the Links, on the Backs, on the Show-park
I oft in memory gaze
It never rained in Peterhead
In the GOOD OLD DAYS.

EARLY SCHOOLDAYS IN THE "BLUE TOON"

THE CHUCKENY SCHOOL

Christmas 1915 - there was a war on or wasn't there? At five years of age the meaning of war was beyond our comprehension, but school was a word we all knew, and now it was our turn. Several of us were 5 ^{1}/2, because we had missed out on the last entry date.

But all was forgotten in the excitement of our first day at school. Proudly carrying our shining new leather bags, containing among other things, a slate (with a sponge on a string), a bottle of water, with Condy's crystals (Potassium Permanganate) a box of "Scallie" (slate pencils) and of course a Playtime piece, we entered the building in which our lives were to be shaped during the next two years.

Hair spruce, bone hard high collar with a neatly knotted tie, long black woollen stockings and shining boots, this was the standard boy's wear. Hair in long ringlets or plaited and beribboned, long pinafore and thick black woollen stockings and again shining black boots, this was the standard girl's outfit.

This was a school which radiated kindness and love for children. The staff were dedicated teachers all, they had to be, when I look back, realising how very poorly paid they were paid. Miss King was the Headmistress, whose awesome presence made even the strongest tremble at the knees. She was a kindly soul and I cannot recall her to even raise her voice.

Of her staff I can remember Miss Smith (Edith), Miss Ingram, Miss Cruickshank and Miss Pyper.

I must mention the size of the classes, about 50 was the usual in those days and handling classes of this size required the best of discipline. I recall the discipline in the "Chuckeny" school was automatic. The above mentioned ladies treated their "Chuckens" as human beings and won their respect and their love.

I often wonder where those "Chuckens" have got to now! Some of them I remember well. I know where some of them are today. Some are dead, and others have gone their separate ways to the ends of the earth.

I can remember John Geddes, John Pope, Alex Ritchie, Bill Birnie and his cousin Andy who lived in the old jail in Prince Street, Jackie Will, Cockets Buchan, Alex Wallace, Charlie Collie, Jimmy Kinnaird, Tom Gibb, Tom Beveridge, Lionel Blow, Henry Relf, Johnnie Matthew, Jim Bruce, Dod Walker from King Street his father was an engine driver, Charlie Gibb, Jimmy Maclean, Danny Summers, Alex Sutherland, John Shuttleton, Emanual Evans (I never did ask him if he was Welsh), Shoddy Reid, Sammy Hill, Sammy Murison, Joe Buchan, Alex Shearer, Alex Mutch, Sandy Scott, Jimmy Wilson, Willie Wilson and Andy Strachan.

I can remember only a few of the girls, Bett Yule, Helen McKenzie, Shena Barclay, Yarta Schultz, Margaret Brown, Annie Walsh, Christian Mess and two Annie Johnstones (I think they were cousins). There were many more but my memory fails me.

One memory that fails me never is the memory of that first day. I can remember distinctly the big wooden rocking horse in the baby room. Oh! the terrible disappointment when I found that rocking on the magnificent beast, while a thrill in anticipation only made me feel horribly sick and Oh so foolish.

The two years at the Infant School sped happily past and little did we dream what a shock was in store for us in our next school, the Central.

CHILDHOOD THOUGHTS

EVENING

Time for bed, lay down your head
Eyes closed tight, just say goodnight
Trust that dawn will bring a waking
Loving hands your shoulder shaking.

AND MORNING

Open wide those heavy eyes
Sleepy head it's time to rise
Wash and dress as quick as able
Breakfast waits you on the table

LIFE IS PRECIOUS

Sleep is over, dawn is breaking
Blackbirds singing, world awaking
Skies are sullen or skies are blue
To be alive is good - how true!

LIFE IN PETERHEAD WHEN THE RESCUE HALL WAS A HOSPITAL

The years of World War 1 were happy years for us. We were too young to know what it was all about and too young to realise that the wounded soldiers who walked our streets in Hospital blue were often young men who would live the rest of their lives under severe handicaps. The Rescue Hall had been turned into a Military Hospital and celebrities such as Dame Clara Butt came to entertain and cheer up our wounded. A gramaphone record of Dame Clara on which she recorded the complete National Anthem was on sale. I had not realised our Anthem had so many verses, I still have one!

The men in Hospital Blue were our heroes, the airmen from Lenabo, who used to collect cigarette cards for us were our heroes, and so were the Sailors from the M.T.B.'s, trawlers and drifters, but our idols were the Sailors from the beautiful yacht the Nairn, which was our special favourite.

I was very young and my memories of the 1st World War are rather disjointed. I can remember how difficult it was to walk "round the harbour" and round the Gadle Braes. Both were heavily guarded because of the Russian Cable which came ashore near the mineral well.

I can remember the Sunday morning my father was arrested as a "Spy". He was on his usual Sunday constitutional round the harbour, after morning service at the Muckle Kirk, and I think he was carrying binoculars this particular Sunday. He was soon released and came home quite enjoying the joke.

I remember Bob Wilson, Mr. Avery (who came from the "Garden" of England, Kent). Sandy Clark, Walter Anderson and the rest of the cable office crew. The cable office was on the top floor of the Post Office building, and the cable crew would open their windows on a warm day. We would do the same, and we played gramophone records for them. One of them was an excellent violonist and another was a flautist.

I can remember tremendous excitement one day when a submarine appeared in the bay. Another day seaplanes appeared on the waters of the bay, but the greatest excitement was the day when a "Blimp" from Lenabo came down in the sea and was hauled on to the embankment by dozens of soldiers.

Another day, one of my brothers and I followed a military (or was it naval) funeral to the old Kirkyard at the links and watched with wide eyes, the rifle firing in tribute to dead enemies. The dead from a sunk U. Boat were being buried and what a scramble there was for the brass cases afterwards!

I can remember the day when no-one would tell us "what was up". Something was obviously very wrong, but no-one would tell us children anything. Adults talking excitedly would "hush up" when we approached. Windows were covered over with heavy curtains and I think blankets. Basins and pails were filled with water or sand and placed at strategic points. I realised later this was when Zeppelins starting raiding the East Coast towns: there must have been a Zeppelin Alert!

I can also recall the time the Russian Warship went ashore near Rattray Head. My father was routed out to act as an interpreter. He had spent a number of years in

Odessa as manager of a Municipal bakery there, and spoke Russian quite well. The Russian's main concern was money, as they had only Russian roubles and kopecs. My father changed quite a sum for them. Out of sentiment he kept this money in his office safe and I remember years later he showed it to me. It was now worthless.

We had a restaurant above the shop as well as one at the back, and we had many friends among the services personnel who frequented them. I can remember at the end of the war a demonstration, on the embankment, of a tank. Compared to the modern tank it was as a flea compared to an elephant, but to us, as it crashed over heaps of rubble and smashed through stone walls, it was an eye opening marvel.

A captured U Boat was on exhibition in the harbour, but we children were not allowed on board, so we had to be content to imagine how it looked downstairs.

GRADUATING FROM THE CHUCKNEY TO THE CENTRAL

The Central School, as I said earlier, gave us quite a shock. I suppose we were supposed to be past the baby stage, and we were expected to react more maturely. When the whistle went at 8.55 a.m. woe betide any boy who was not already in the playground. If not, you were late and lined up outside the boy's entrance. There, you had to shake hands with the male assistant and say "Thank you!" In those days, he was a huge man. When you had done this, and were now in tears, your punishment was not over. You then proceeded upstairs to line up outside room 1 and there this terrifying figure of the male assistant would walk along the line, dishing out clinical doses of the "Lochgelly". All this time he wore a huge grin. Apparently to him it was all a great joke. It was no joke to his victims. The "goodies" who were not late had by this time lined up in the playground class by class, like soldiers they were called smartly to attention, and, one class at a time, they marched smartly round the corner and into the boy's entrance. As we entered, we heard what seemed at first discordant noises, but later turned out to be two pianos, each thumping out a march tune. One was in the hall and was for the downstairs classes and the other was on the balcony and was for the seniors. This could be quite confusing, because the two pianos were generally offering two different tunes.

The Headmaster at this time was a gentleman named Mr. Reid. We did not see very much of him, as he seemed to leave most of the day to day running of the school to his staff. However I do have one rather vivid memory of this gentleman. I think our class teacher at this time was a Miss Davidson (or was its Mrs.?) We were in room 14 at the time, and from where I sat I had a very good view of the balcony near room 1. On this particular day ours studies were rudely interrupted by a "hullabaloo" upstairs. I could see a woman (I can remember her very well, even her name) with a shawl over her head, arms waving about wildly, and her voiced raised in screaming anger. Mr. Reid suddenly appeared and tried to pacify her. All I can remember of what followed was a sudden and explosive tableau. The woman suddenly bent down and snatching off a shoe "sent it flying" at Mr. Reid's head. We saw no more, because by this time, our teacher, realising we were all gaping, brought us quickly back to earth, and our attention back to her lesson.

7

Of the Central school I have many happy memories, and a few not so happy. I can remember the arrival of Mr. McLean our new Headmaster. I think he came from Fochabers? I know he was a very kindly gentleman, although, like his predecessor he was a strict disciplinarian. I remember Miss Hutchison (Nellie) who taught pianoforte, and who used to rap my fingers with her pencil when I persistently played a wrong note. One of my happiest memories is when our new male assistant arrived, a Mr. Edgar. He started a football team. Sandy Ritchie was goalkeeper, and "Memo" Guilianotti was centre forward. Andy Bruce and Jim Bruce - the others are just faces without names. At this time although I was football daft, I had "two left feet" and did not make the team.

Upstairs was a "lady" teacher who once sent me home with a "black eye". We were lined up to dismiss. The "privileged" one opened the door and fastened it back, and everyone shuffled back. Someone shuffled back on to my toes, and I must have exclaimed, because I got the back of the teacher's hand across my face. A cameo ring gave me the most beautiful "blue keeker" which lasted a week or more.

The only time I can remember my mother really angry was when I came home with this decoration and explained how I got it.

I can remember "Belle Middleton" who once told me she could dip hen's claws in ink and get better writing from the hen than she got from me. I think she said the same thing to Charlie Collie. She was quite right, although I often wonder how anyone ever managed to write neatly with those J pens. I kept some of them for years just to remind myself. Heaven help anyone with a blot on a copy book! I can also remember a Miss Dawson (Paraffin Kate), her father delivered paraffin, a Miss Cran and a Miss Allan (her father was a stationmaster).

Those were hungry days, days of mass unemployment and ragged bootless children. At playtime those with a playtime piece were often besieged by less fortunate pals asking for a bite.

In the winter, if we had snow, it was an adventure reaching school. Prince Street would be crowded at lunchtime by Central school boys snowballing "Academy Rats" or "Northers" waylaying solitary Central school boys. All this was very serious, and believe me, at 8 or 9 years of age it could be very terrifying too.

All arguments between boys were settled after school "up the lanie" and some bloody battles took place. The lane ran from King Street (next to Pow Tam's) and came out opposite the girl's door in Prince Street. Although most fights took place there, occasionally one which could not wait, took place in an opening opposite the boy's gate next to Campbell's garage. In this case the chances were the fight was discovered and the combatants thrashed "a la Lochgelly!" Very rarely did a fight start in the playground. Few would have dared.

With the introduction of school football a much better "pupil-teacher" relationship developed, certainly with the boys, and those in the school team became the envy of the other fellows.

PETERHEAD ACADEMY (THE HOUSE BUILT UPON A ROCK)

DOMUS SUPER PETRAM

The house that is upon a rock
Sure builded cannot fall
The rock of knowledge and of God
That answers every call
To every corner sends her sons
And daughters fit to lead
In every clime, in every sphere
In very word and deed
DOMUS DOMUS DOMUS
SUPER PETRAM AEDIFICATA.

From humble homes, from croft and close
It's granite walls embrace
And nourish and sustain the flame
And keep it in its place
It shall not be extinguished but
Rather shall increase
So long as God's in Heaven and until
Ugie's waters cease.
DOMUS DOMUS DOMUS
SUPER PETRAM AEDIFICATA.

EAGLE JEAN - BABBY - MADAM - PA RICE

Soon - far too soon - it was time to go up to the Academy. We all wanted to go there, but so many horrifying tales had been told about the initiation ceremonies on your first day, that we were nearly all a "wee bit" scared. Actually, our first day proved to be quite uneventful and we soon settled down to the new routine.

New faces, new names, "Eagle Jean" - "Babbie", "Bathie", and "Buckie" and "Madam" to name but a few. I must, of course mention the "daddy" of them all. "pa" - the Rector, Mr. Rice, affectionately known to all as "Pa", one of the most gentlemanly people it has been my privelage to know. His elegant figure in top hat and tailcoat, striding down York Street homeward bound, is a sight many generations will recall with pleasure.

"Eagle Jean" - Eagle, I suppose, because, just as an eagle can see a fish from way up high, Miss Jean could spot the slightest misdemeanour from any corner of the room, and, believe me her acid tongue could shrivel up even the toughest.

"Babbie" a kindly soul, in some ways, but "slightly past it". It was quite common for her to put her feet up on the front desk and to fall fast asleep in the middle of a lesson. We were not surprised since her subject was rather dry, (Latin).

"Bathie" - how we did tease her! I remember one day, she became rather annoyed and threw the wooden duster at one of the boys. Her aim was rather poor and, the duster hit "poor unsuspecting Gordon Hislop" who was sitting in front of the real culprit. Gordon, quite indignant, refused to retrieve the duster when ordered. We were quite amazed because Gordon was such a quiet boy.

"Madam", as the name implies, taught French (and German) but, as the name also implies, she had very fixed ideas, and was very determined to get her own way. She met her match, however, in Marion Forest. Madam always wore long skirts, and insisted that the girls showed as little leg as humanly possible. To show knees was unforgivable, but Marion was determined she and her classmates would show their knees if they wished to. The girls, under Marion's guidance, raised their gym slips to the last notch, but under Madam's sharp eye, they were marched to the nearest cloakroom, and were ordered to let down their slips. They obediently did so, and were promptly marched back to the classroom. At Marion's instigation, by the time they reached the classroom, all the slips were hitched up again as far as they would go.

"Buckie" as well as classics master, was sportsmaster, and the boys adored him. He had a permanent cough, and kept popping out of class and round the corner (there was a staff room near his classroom and of course the inevitable rumours said he kept a stock of "cough mixture" there). This is where I must tell the story of Peterhead Celtic F.C.

I had a photograph of the Celtic team, but, after my one and only visit from Dave Massie (he came home once only from Hudson Bay) I'm afraid I never saw that photograph again!

ON THE BALL WITH PETERHEAD CELTIC!

I said earlier that I had two left feet and so I did not make the Central School Football Team. Later I discovered I had two very "safe" hands, and exceptionally quick reflexes, in simple language, I discovered I could play even with two left feet - I could play in goal. Tom Beveridge, Charlie Collie and I used to play at Forehill (Waterworks) on the grass, and there I learned to sprawl out and dive for a football without hurt or bruise. Tom used to spend his summer holidays at Forehill, and Charlie and I used to visit frequently.

As a result of this I "made" the Academy Junior team, but when we were too old for it, we were still too young for the Academy Senior team, and there were two years of a gap. It was because of this that the Peterhead Celtic was born. Tom Beveridge,

"Curly" Smith, "Shoddy" Reid, "Barry" Brown, Harold Webster, "Doddy" Forest, Dave Massie and I found ourselves with no team to play for, and since we were all football daft, this had to be put right. We got hold of a few lads who had left school, such as John Mitchell and Jack Simpson, and, clubbing our resources together we bought a football (an improved "T" cost £1) and a set of jerseys.

We chose the green and white hoops and the name Celtic, don't ask me why, but one thing I can say, we certainly did not disgrace either the name or the jerseys. We must have played for two seasons at least, and we never lost a match, indeed I do not think we even drew a game. As far as I can remember we won the lot - but the game we all wanted to play - against the only team we had not met, and who were about our own strength - was never played. We challenged the Academy Senior team, and they were keen to play us, because the whole youth of the town were divided, some said the Celtic would wipe the floor with the Academy team whilst others said the reverse.

This climax to two seasons rivalry was very nearly achieved. Since "Buckie" refused to sanction such a game, the Academy Senior team agreed secretly to play us on our "home" pitch at the Links. They duly appeared and stripped and were about to take the field, when, striding over the Links from Cairntrodlie came "Buckie". He was furious and ordered the Academy Seniors home, so, the game was never played. Next season, however, all the Celtic players who were still at school, played for the Academy first eleven. I can remember one Monday - it was an Aberdeen holiday - and an Aberdeen Boys Brigade team had arranged to play Peterhead Boys Brigade at Raemoss Park after school. Raemoss had not been levelled or drained at this time, and it had been raining heavily. Raemoss was a quagmire. I was a spectator, dressed in my school clothes. If I remember rightly, I was in a new parson grey suit with long trousers. As luck would have it (bad luck) the local team had no goalkeeper, and I agreed to play, on condition that I was allowed to go home to change. The B.B.'s insisted there was no time, and eventually I agreed to play. By the end of the game, I was caked in mud from head to toe - and I had retrieved the ball from the back of the net no less than nine times. Next day I was told "Buckie" and the school captain - either Ian Findlay or Sandy Chalmers - had watched the game and my name duly appeared on the team sheet for next Saturdays first eleven game. It was at Inverurie and I can remember it to this day. What a thrill - to play for the school first team - and - what a shock to hear one day in the seventies - my old school team turned out against Inverurie Academy, with only nine players. What a disgrace for a school of this size and reputation - I really felt miserable when I heard.

To return to the 1920's four of the Academy first eleven played trials for Peterhead F.C. "Curly" Smith, Bruce Findlay, Dave Massie and myself. Dave and I eventually signed for Peterhead as also did "Doddy" Forest. Dave could have made it in any grade but he chose to go and work for the Hudson Bay Co. My own senior career was a very short one, terminated by a motor bicycle accident, in which I was quite seriously injured.

"Doddie" Forest played for Plymouth Argyll. Of the Celtic F.C. Jimmy Kinnaird was killed in the bombing of Hall Russels shipyard, John Mitchell went to Hudson Bay as did Jack Simpson, John was drowned in a canoeing accident. "Doddie" Forest I think is in Africa, "Barry" Brown I think is still in Peterhead. Tom Beveridge and Shoddy Reid are dead, and Dave Massie has also passed on. He came home only once from Canada, and spent a day with me in Port Elphinstone. He spent most of the day playing football with my son Pat. Of the others I have lost trace completely, but I cannot end the story of the Celtic without mentioning the teams mascots. We had two originally, Georgie Barclay - who never missed a game, and who became a banker, and Garden West who seldom missed a game. Later on we had George Mair who became my "twin" and was always between the sticks with me at practice. He became Peterhead goalkeeper and played for a Scottish First Division team (I think Queen of the South). This was of course, before the days of the Premier League.

Amongst our regular opponents was a team against whom we played always on New Years morning. "Bappies" ran this team, I do not remember his proper name. I think he was from the Roanheads.

THE HIGHERS

Not a sound was heard, not a single note,
As they sat in the Exam Hall and sweated,
Many a mind was cast back with a lump in the throat,
As the oft wasted hours were regretted.

"If only I'd thought, if only I'd known,
I'd have spent those hours with more profit,
If only I'd known - but no use to moan,
I'll just do my best and then "hop it".

THE PETERHEAD SCOUTS IN THE TWENTIES

The Scouts met in the old school in St. Peter Street (the soup kitchen) opposite "Jimmy Sutherlands". Shortly after I joined we moved to Wilson Street (later to be the J.I.C.). "Middy" was a scoutmaster, Donald Sutherland and Johnny Buchan were his assistants, and Jimmy Geddes was bandmaster. Oh yes! we had a scout band in those days, resplendently equipped with shining brass bugles, kettle drums and a big drum, all supplied by Mr. and Mrs. Butcher. Church parades were led by the band, and in the summer we marched - yes marched! behind our bugle band to Blackhills where we always camped. Mr. Robertson, who had a dairy farm there, always made us very welcome. I can remember the band and some of the bugle music, but most clearly of all I can still picture "Mutt and Jeff", two brothers, one of whom was so tall that he was a natural for the big drum - so he was the big drummer.

We always left for camp on a Saturday afternoon, and I had always a bag of Nicol's pies in my knapsack. Our first stop was always at the corner just beyond Dales and there we had a good feed to help us on our way. At camp we built our own cookhouse, and did all our own cooking etc. Each patrol took its turn, day about, on "fatigue" duty. This consisted of cooking, cleaning, gathering firewood, and keeping a huge barrel at the cookhouse door filled with clean, cool fresh water. This barrel, on my first fatigue day reminded me of the "Widow's Cruise" - but in reverse - it would not fill! Another tenderfoot and I spent most of the day walking to and from the well, which seemed miles away, carrying pails of water, trying to keep that barrel full - Happy days - and nights. We would go on midnight patrols and manoeuvres. One side defending the camp - the other side attempting to capture the camp flag. At the end, steaming mugs of cocoa, and "farthing biscuits" - in those days they were a mouthful not a nibble like our present day "butter hard".

The days were spent in woodcraft and nature expeditions - making gadgets such as bridges, swings, boot-racks, plate-racks etc. On a wet night we would slip out under the flies, and tighten our neighbour's guy ropes, and wait expectantly for the roars of dismay when their tent pole burst through the apex of their tent, and a patrol was buried under a heap of wet canvas. I remember one year half of the camp was flooded out the first night by a fierce thunder storm. It was all great fun, they rescued their bedding etc. and moved into a hay loft in the farm. They spent a most enjoyable night sleeping in the hay. Everything was dried out next day, and the camp was resumed.

The camp concert was great fun. I remember Middy used to star as one of "Harry Gordon's" auld wifies. He was ably supported by Johnny Buchan and Donald Sutherland. The Blackhills people always turned out in force to our concerts.

Mention of the scout band brings back memories of other bands in Peterhead. No - one can ever forget the Salvation Army Band, which paraded every Sunday morning and played beautifully at several different places in the town. When you heard the Salvation Army Band playing a bright, brisk march on their way back to the Citadel, you knew you should be well on your way to the "Kirk" if you were not to be late.

The other band I remember well was the Aberdeen Boy's Brigade Band which used to visit Peterhead, I think annually, to lead a Church Parade. Their big drummer was the envy of all us wee laddies. Not only was he allowed to whack the big drum - but he wore a leopard skin - and this made our eyes "goggle".

PETERHEAD BOY SCOUTS
1923

THE HEYDAY OF JIMMY SUTHERLAND

A book could be written about Jimmy Sutherland. In business he could be ruthless. He ran nearly all his rivals in the "bus business" off the road. But there was another side to Jimmy which we young lads were quick to exploit. If we wished to hire a bus to Pittodrie for a "big" match, we would approach Jimmy personally - always personally! "How much for a 32 seater to Pittodrie on Saturday Jimmy?" Jimmy would say "Oh make it two pounds!" "Well" we would reply "Burnett has offered us 35/- (175p)", quick as a flash Jimmy would say, "30/- (150p)". I've seen him say one pound - he could not bear to be beaten by one of his rivals especially Burnett - Mintlaw! Of course he must have known we were having him in on, but we still got the bus.

I've known him put on a special bus to take someone in to Aberdeen if they had missed the last bus. I remember one day counting more than fifty people in a 32 seater bus coming home from Aberdeen. Jimmy would never willingly leave anyone behind, and his drivers knew it! I have one vivid memory of an incident in one of Jimmy's buses. It was during the war, and I was returning, with my wife and family to Peterhead on holiday. It was a double-decker and we were approaching the top of Stirling Hill when there was an almighty explosion, and the bus swung wildly across the road. I can see the driver yet! feet up against the door! both hands on the wheel - sweat pouring down his face as he successfully pulled the bus to a stop on the safe side of the road! Our immediate thought was we had been bombed! But it was a "blow-out", a front wheel

14

at that! How the driver kept the bus on the road I'll never know.

THE "ORRA" LOON

He starte't in the mornin, afore the sin cam ower the hill,
An fin the sin wis doon, 'twis dark, bit he wis tyavin still,
He chappe't neeps an ither jobs - he even barr'ed muck,
Fae Monday morn till Monday morn - half day? He'd nae sic luck!
His claes wis fae the fairmer's wife, twis ony cast aff cloots,
His feet wis sair - they hid tae be wi weerin hand-doon boots.
A smilin face he aye hid on, an niver did he say,
A wird agin a sowl, altho he felt like mony a day,
He worket hard, come rain or sleet or snaw,
He learnt a lot 0 fairmin - in time he kent it a,
Oor Jock wis nay a feel - tho he wis treated like een files,
He saved up ivry bawbee, niver went oot on the tiles,
An noo he's made his wye in life, a placie o his ain,
A wife an bairns, a cosy hoos, he'll niver be alane.
The moral is hoo-iver low ye start, if ye wint up,
It's up ye'll go if ye jist try, aye richt up tae the top!

THE PETERHEAD ACADEMY TEAM IN THE TWENTIES!

The team photo shows the Academy Football team I think in 1926. From left to right - Back row - Charlie Collie, R. L. Richards, Jimmy Kinnaird, Ernie Strachan, P. L. Nicol, Ian Thomson (New Deer), Tom Beveridge, Ben Collie, Norman Lawrie. Front row - W. T. Buchanan (Buckie), Curly Smith, Ian Cardno, George Cowie (Capt.), David Massie, Bruce Findlay, and The Rector Mr. C. D. Rice.

George Cowie our Captain, believed in shouting all the time, and he left you in no doubts as to what he thought you should have done, and what he actually thought about what you had done! He was a very good captain and very well liked! Jimmy Kinnaird was a very stubborn, determined defender and very few wingers got past his strong tackling.

Bruce Findlay was a very polished wing half. He played trials for Peterhead senior team, and undoubtedly would have made the senior grade had he not had one weak knee. I had one too, and when Bruce's knee went he would shout for me, and with one hand under his heel and the other above his knee if it did not go back with the first swing it generally went back with the second. Crude - sore - but effective, and Bruce would stamp his foot, shout "OK ref!" and carry on as if it had never happened.

Ian Thomson was the son of the Headmaster of New Deer School. He played left back, and the next year he was to have as a partner, another Ian Thomson, this one the son of "Cocky Thomson!"

Curly Smith was a really classy wing half, or inside forward, a brother of Andrew Smith. He also played trials for Peterhead. His lack of weight was his only defect.

Ian Cardno was the left winger - a speed merchant who could also snap goals.

David Massie could turn his hands (and feet) to anything! He was good at everything he tried - Tennis, Badminton, Bowls - you name it - he could play it! He was a right winger and he was right in the Alex Jackson mould. Very fast, and with a shot like a cannon ball. He could have made the first division seniors had he not chosen to go to Hudson Bay, where he became a Post Manager!

PETERHEAD ACADEMY FOOTBALL TEAM

From left to right - Back row - Charlie Collie, R. L. Richards, Jimmy Kinnaird,
Ernie Strachan, P. L. Nicol, Ian Thomson (New Deer), Tom Beveridge, Ben Collie, Norman Lawrie.
Front row - W. T. Buchanan (Buckie), Curly Smith, Ian Cardno, George Cowie (Capt.), David Massie, Bruce
Findlay, and The Rector Mr. C. D. Rice.

PLAYTIME IN PETERHEAD IN THE TWENTIES!

We hear so often from the young these days "I'm bored!" In our young days in Peterhead we were never bored. We could always find something to do. We made our own amusements, and quite often equipment too!

One of our favourite playgrounds was the lower end of Prince Street, another was the bottom end of St, Mary Street. Jimmy Kinnaird lived at the corner of St. Mary Street and St. Peter Street. Tom Gibb lived in a flat above Jimmy and Tom Beveridge who lived in the house beside the lane into Eddie Lumsden's workshop - so this area was a natural for a playground. In that same lane, someone made candy. I can't remember who, but a special treat occasionally in the Central school playground was when "burnt candy" was lowered over the wall during "playtime" in a pail.

If we tired of the street, we often went up to the "little parkie" in Landale Road. It is now the municipal gardens. In those days it was a grass field, used by the fishermen to dry nets, and so it had the added attraction for us - the small corks, used to float the nets, were used by all the boys for football and of course the cast-off nets were always great play things. I remember one day for example, we found a bundle of torn and tangled nets in the "parkie". We tied it on the end of a piece of rope, and arranged a fishing expedition! We went over "the queenie" to the "backs" where we trawled all the inlets in the rocks. We only caught sticklebacks, but that was good enough. Thinking they would make good pets we put them in some jars and took them home, but alas! they died. When we were older the "backs" and the "garron" were favourite fishing places. A length of string, some "four a penny hooks", a piece of lead and some old herrings, and you were set! On a good day we would catch dozens of "poddies" and "saithe!"

In later years my older brother Jim often took me out on the bay fishing. We could hire a rowing boat, with fishing lines (and even bait supplied) for sixpence an hour (2½p). We had a favourite spot. Part of the finding of this spot was to line up the town house spire with something or other, I can't remember what exactly, but I do remember we used to catch "dabs", whiting, podlies and an occasional haddock, plaice or cod, and if we were lucky sometimes a shoal of mackerel entered the bay and then the fun was fast and furious. I remember once we went out with a Mr. Philip, Merchant Street, in his motor boat, (his brother was a partner in Philip and Buchan, drapers in Thistle Street). On this occasion we had an exciting catch! Someone brought up quite a large squid! It attached itself to the deck so firmly that Mr. Philip had to kick and kick hard with his sea boots to dislodge it.

As a special treat I was occasionally allowed out with the older boys, on Mr. Strachan's boat from Buchanhaven. Most people will remember the Strachan boys Beau, Beezer and Andy, all footballers for Buchanhaven Hearts, and one or was it two of them played also for the Peterhead senior team. This was really exciting fishing! We had a heavy iron triangle, with six or was it nine hooks, baited with lug worms. You lowered the triangle till it hit bottom, and then raised it a few inches and waited. What a thrill to pull up your line with three or four flat fish hooked, and hard work too!

17

On another occasion I went cod fishing out on the rocks near the slaughter house. The idea was to go out as far as you could on the rocks, when the tide was out, and fish, and retreat gradually as the tide came in. The bait used was "saftens" that is crabs which had shed their shell. These were gathered the day before, and I well remember the first time I went. I brought a tin for my "saftens". My fisherman friend just lifted his "Bunnet", put each crab inside it and replaced his headgear. This could be quite exciting fishing, but not to be recommended. It could be very dangerous!

My father's foreman baker was the best rod fisher I have ever watched! Many people will remember Jimmy Macintosh, who knew the River Ugie probably better than anyone else in his day. He took me once or twice to the entrance to the North Harbour (now closed up). Here he would fish for Lythe. The fish was very like Salmon. He used "Sunnel" (sand eels) which he would wriggle enticingly across the surface of the water. The Lythe re-acted almost exactly like a Salmon. I used to admire the ease with which Jimmy could cast a fly, and his accuracy! With a fifteen foot Greenheart, he could land a fly "on a sixpence!" on the widest stretches of the Ugies tidal reaches, and on a windy day too!

I mentioned the "Little Parkie", other favourite "Parkies" were the "show park" (now the public bowling greens, tennis courts etc.) Raemoss Park, now levelled and drained, and of course our short cut to the golf course, Baird's Parks, the land at the top of Hope Street, now completely built over, and although Mr. Baird used to chase us for our lives, we still used this short cut regularly. A favourite spot of ours was the "little linkies" opposite the War Memorial, where the grassy slopes down to the rocks were broken with innumerable sand holes. Here, and on the rocks below, where old drifters had been wedged to be broken up, we could spend whole afternoons, sometimes playing "cowboys and indians", sometimes we were pirates and just as often we just explored the rock pools or gathered limpets, which we roasted. We would gather driftwood and seaweed, build a fire and place a flat piece of iron on top like a girdle, and roast the limpets on it. I never could abide the taste of them, nor of the "Buckies" (whelks) which we boiled in a tin of sea water.

Often when the school broke for easter, the first fine day, was a picnic day! Off we would go, armed with buns, "ale" and ropes. Sometimes we went to the "fower plantins" (a crossroad on the old Inverugie road, which had trees at each corner) or occasionally we would venture further afield and go to the "pinkie braes". This was the grassy slopes down to the Ugie near the Cruives. There we would be a Tarzan, swinging on the trees or cowboys or indians or highwaymen. No-one ever bothered us. We had a tremendous freedom in these places which I think young people today are denied!

LIVE!

Life is short, and memory shorter still,
So! live life well, and live it to the fill,
For - come the day the last trump sounds,
For you - sweet nothing-ness abounds!

ODOURS - APPETISING AND OTHERWISE!

In the summer evenings a most appetising odour would blanket some areas of the town - the kipperers were busy! The herring is the KING of fish, there is no tastier fish to be found! Whether it be in salt water or fresh!, and probably the tastiest form of it is the kipper! I mean of course the real kipper - the smoked variety, not the dyed substitute so often offered today! And the best way to cook a kipper is to cook it in the kiln among the smouldering oak chips with which it was cured! Johnny Buchan, one of our scoutmasters owned a kippering yard, at Keith Inch, over the "Queenie". There on a summer evening, you could eat a kipper newly smoked and newly cooked in the smouldering oak chips in the kiln. The very thought of it makes my mouth water!

"Gentry" from the Cruden Bay Railway Hotel used to dine on kippers regularly in the Keith Inch yard!

After my brother Jackie went to Glasgow, I used to send him a half-box of kippers (approximately 36 kippers) in the post , I think the total cost was two shillings and nine pence old money, (approximately 14p in today's currency!) Johnnies "gaffer" was an old classmate of mine, Joe Buchan.

Oh! I started with an enticing odour, I'll finish off with the opposite, again in high summer, but this time on the embankment or near any curing yard - the stench was unbelievable - but we seldomed noticed it because the girls whose nimble fingers wielded razor sharp knives so swiftly you could not follow their movements, sang, laughed and joked, all the time they worked. If they were so happy, why should we complain?

AND CAMPING!

For several years, a group of us camped out at Whitehills, in a small wood. There were David Massie, Curly Smith, "Barry" Brown, and I at one end of the wood, and at the other end was a camp of older boys, "Smiddy" Ritchie, "Ceggies" Carnegie, ? Shearer and other members of Peterhead Y.M.C.A.

I remember we always borrowed a horse and cart from "Shoddy" Reid's father, and. loaded with a couple of old beds, a bell tent, kettles, pans etc. we would drive out on the Easter Saturday morning, and set up camp!

On week days we would cycle into school in the morning. We had a high trapeze, ropes for climbing, and all sorts of gadgets, all home made of course! We built a fireplace and did all our own cooking. This could be quite tricky in wet weather, but we throve on this life, and we certainly learned to look after ourselves. It was about this time that some of our class-mates started to go "caddying" at Cruden Bay golf course. They cycled out, caddied for two rounds, and cycled home agin for 1/3 per round (7p). It was a hard life, but a healthy one. It could also be a profitable one if you were lucky.

One lucky one was John Shuttleton. He was a bright scholar, indeed he was Academy

Dux, specialising in French and German! He caddied one day for Sir Jeremiah Coleman (of mustard fame). They became good friends, and John was offered a job with Sir Jeremiah's company!

The Cruden Bay tournament was a great affair. The railway company Hotel was always full and the tournament attracted all the leading amateur golfers of the day such as Dr. Clelland, Dr. Brown. Sandy Grossert, and Bertie Brand and such like! Then there was "Horsie" night when the "Horses" were drawn, and those lucky enough to draw a "Horsie" (a player who had qualified), in the sweepstake could sell their "Horsie" to the highest bidder. A successful Cruden Bay tournament meant of course a successful Peterhead one too, because it was held the week after, and most of the golfers stayed on for both!

At that time we had a few local cracks as well, such as Jack Robertson, Fred Wernham, Connon Johnstone etc. I remember Jack Robertson was particularly good with the "cleek" (equivalent to a number one iron, and undoubtedly the most difficult club to play). I caddied for him in several tournaments!

DRIFTERS, COAL HEAVERS AND "RUNNERS!"

Kippers and then golf tournaments - what a mixture! Lets return to the kippers, or rather to their origin!, the herring drifter! I can recall summers when one could almost walk across the South Harbour from drifter to drifter, (and anyone falling in might drown, today anyone falling in would be more likely to be poisoned or choked by rubbish!) We would marvel at the dexterity and brute strength of the coal-heavers. When a drifter had landed its "shot" when its nets had been rushed away to dry slung over the railings in Catto Drive, or spread out round some fields or other, then the coal lorries would come bustling down. Wooden planks were laid from the quay to the nearest drifter and then from drifter to drifter. The manhole covers over the coal bunkers on deck were lifted, and then the coal-heavers got to work. With an empty coal-sack over their shoulders and a Cwt sack of coal on their backs, they would actually run on board the drifters and heave the bag upside down, aiming the small opening with unnerving accuracy! It was a particularly tricky job if the tide was out since this meant a fearful slope from the quay to the first drifter. I never yet so a coal-heaver slip!

In the early morning the first drifters would appear, and immediately a race started from the harbour to the other end of the town, Buchanhaven, Roanheads, Hay Crescent, Victoria Road etc. where the skippers lived, boys racing to tell the skippers wives their man's boat was in with a "shottie". You could tell when a boat came into the bay, if her nets were up, or if she was low in the water, but as she entered the harbour the crew would signal the boys, giving the actual number of crans, and one member of the crew would jump ashore with a "kit" containing a sample for the sale room! A "tanner" reward for saying a "shot" could become a half-crown for saying 50-80, or even 100 crans! (a cran was four baskets).

I became very friendly with the skipper of P.D.5 "The Quicksand". Her skipper was Sandy Ritchie's father, and part of her crew comprised the Inverallochy golfers who played against a team of M.P.'s and who went down to the House of Commons on a visit!

They tried me hard to come out for a night's fishing with them, but since I was a rotten sailor, I never went. Years later, I put my name down at "Varsity" for a trip on a trawler. There were approximately 100 names, and I was egged on "You'll never be chosen!" I was, and a 4 a.m. one Saturday morning, I arrived at the quayside at Aberdeen Harbour, and lo and behold! the trawler was none other than my old friend the Peterhead drifter "City of Edinburgh". By the time we crossed the "bar" I was sick, and by the time the trawl was shot, I was so ill I took no further interest until we had tied up again in the harbour!

THE DEMON DRINK

As a youngster In Peterhead I can recall many elections, political ones, when the blind M.P. Fred Martin of St. Dunstans Mintlaw, held the N.E. constituency for the Liberals against all comers. That was until that "kenspeckle figure", Baillie Booth of Downiehills discovered that promising youngster Bob Boothby. Boothby, whose gravelly voice seemed to boom out from his boots to reach every member of his audience. Boothby, whose quick wit and masterly repartee won over even his party's bitterest opponents. Town Council elections with such figures as Provost Leask, Provost Dickie, Baillie Dingwall, Baillie Duncan and Baillie Nicol (my father).

But the elections which standout most in my memory were elections in which no-one was elected to any post political or municipal. Amongst the fishing community there was a very strong element who were "Tee Total" and forced the Town council to hold regular elections. In these the towns people were given three choices -
1. they could vote for prohibition.
2. they could vote for limitation.
3. they could vote for No Change.

These election campaigns were carried out with great fervour and led to lively arguments throughout the town. It was rounded off with a grand procession through the main streets of the town, carrying banners depicting the evils of drinking. A pal of mine worked in John E. Hutchison's shop in Queen Street. It was a licensed grocer shop and my pal told me that as the procession passed several "wifies" dropped out and came into the back door carrying a basket, asking him to slip a "bottlie" intae ma basket for medicine of course, because after the election there would be no more alcohol sold in Peterhead. To the best of my recollection the result was usually a win for Limitation, so that for quite a period of years the number of public house licences was whittled away. The magistrates , whose unpopular task it was to decide which licenses should be cancelled, made a serious miscalculation here, one which was to cost the town dear. They cancelled the licenses of all the "pubs" around the harbour area, until there was not one single "pub" along the harbour front. During the herring fishing, June and July, hundreds of drifters from North and South Shields and from Yarmouth and Lowestoft crowded the Peterhead harbours. Now the English fishermen, unlike their Scottish counterparts, loved their beer. When a drifter was ready for sea, all the skipper had to do was send a messenger around the harbour front to summon his crew. Now with no "pubs" along the harbour, it became more and more difficult to reach his men who had now to go up town for a drink. The solution to this problem was a simple one. Most of the English drifters now chose to fish from Fraserburgh, and in a few years time Peterhead had only a sprinkling of English vessels.

The temperance parades I spoke of usually ended up with a meeting on the links, where the crowd was harangued by vehement "tub thumpers" ranting on about the evils of drink.

> Hyterin, Styterin, fu as a Lord,
> He's drunk far mair than he can afford,
> His cares are gone - at least till the morn,
> Nae mair dis he feel lost or forlorn.
>
> Bye the "nick" - he's safely past,
> Afa nearly hame at last,
> A rude awaknin he will get,
> Fan he comes thru his ain front yette.
>
> Instead o supper he'll be stung,
> His wife awaits wi a real het tongue,
> She's hid HER maet, aye lang ago,
> She's nae keepin his het - no, no, no.
>
> The kye-hole on the door's gye sma,
> It winna bide still, nae ava,
> The kye gaes skliterin doon the path,
> That jist delays the gweed wife's wrath.
>
> A kindly neebor passin bye,
> Peer Willum's dilemma did espy,
> "Here man see if I can help"
> Bit Willum gaed him sik a skelp

Then Willum fell flat on his face,
A neebor said " oh sic disgrace",
We're in a high class pairt o toon,
The gommeril's nae half let us doon.

Wi that the door flew open wide,
An Willum's gweed wife stepped ootside,
"Get up ye drunken stinkin' sot",
Peer Willum tried - but not alot.

His feet, they widna haud the grun,
His heed wis birlin - wyed a ton,
He tried tae rise, he tried tae creep,
Then losh behere - he fell asleep.

The simple moral's seldom learn't,
If you are oot on pleasure bent,
Nivir drink mair than ye need,
The morn ye'll rue the silly deed!

Other meetings on the links I can remember were meetings held during a "revival",
that was a religious revival. These occurred periodically. A preacher would arrive from
the "South" and meetings would be held on the links. A small harmonium would be
set up, and leaflets handed out with the words of well known "Sanky" hymns such as
"Shall We Gather At The River". These hymns had wonderfully rousing tunes, and
soon the crowd would be worked up into a religious fervour and ready to be harangued
by the preacher. He left them in no doubt that they were the world's worst sinners, and
if there had been a bad fishing then that was their punishment. Many poor souls were
carried away and took this to heart. It was quite common for someone to be so carried
away they fainted.

What on earth is it all about?
Those who think they know all shout,
Salvation! The blood of Christ alone,
Can bring you to that awful throne,
Where judgment then shall be dispensed, ✗
If black (or white) then life eternal,
If red beware, then fires infernal,
Robbie Burns warned Tam O Shanter,
Robbie ayeways loved tae banter,
"In Hell they'll roast ye" he warned Tam,
Tho Rab himsel neer cared a damn,
after" dispensed " For "pentance stools" nor Hell's damnation
These he deemed imagination.

Your whole life in one 23 page condensed

"Love thy neighbour, help each other,
Treat each man he were your brother.
Hold your head high, enjoy life,
Live at peace, avoiding strife."

SUNDAY "PROTICKS"

The Sunday "appetiser" was traditional. After the morning service at the "Muckle Kirk", mothers went home to see to the lunch, and fathers went for an appetising walk, always round the "embankment" and round the harbour. After this it might vary slightly. If Mr. Swans sermon was a little longer or if it was a communion service which did last longer, the walk might be ended in the Seagate, with a short cut up the Backgate which got them home in time.

"The Muckle Kirk"

On a nice Sunday morning, if there was plenty of time, the walk would extend round the "Wickets", and even round the Gadle Braes. I'll never forget one particular Sunday. We youngsters had Sunday School after the morning service, and we had only time for a quick "dander" round the harbour and home. This day we were picking up small stones and tossing them up in the air. As they came down, we kicked them to see who could kick one the furthest. I had on my new Sunday (Little Duke) boots - the first time on - and was my face red? I kicked one boot right over the nearest drifter and splash into the harbour!

There I was, with one boot on, otherwise in my Sunday best, not knowing whether to weep or join in the laughter of my companions! Eventually I hirpled round to "Collie" the druggist (Simpsons, Longate branch) and sat in the shop till Charlie went home for another pair of boots for me. I'll not say what happened next. It was too painful.

THE SUNDAY THE LAIRD FELL ASLEEP!

The meenister's sermon wis gey dry,
An seen the Laird wis heard tae sigh,
Sine aifter at his heid gaed doon,
Then "losh be-here" Oh sicken a soon!

His snorin wid a droon't a band,
Gweed luck the beedle wis at hand,
"Up here Sandy" the meenister cried,
Up the pulpit stairs auld Sandy hied,

"The Laird ye'll hae tae gie a shak
His snorin I jist canna tak,
My ain wird I canna hear,
Ye'll hae tae waukin him up I fear".

"Weel meenister, jist ye harkin tae me,
I think, at even ye'll agree,
Twis you pit the Laird tae sleep doon there,
So ye'd better waukin im up - fairs fair!"

"BUTTERIES" AND FOOTBALL!

Every morning my brother Jack and I delivered "butteries" for the shop. What a job my father had getting us up out of bed! On Saturdays we were message boys all day, and the Saturday afternoon delivery was to Buchanhaven. Big Jim Watt, Bill Mackintosh (later of Mackintosh Brothers), Jackie and I would set off for Buchanhaven pushing "Hurlies" packed with loaves, buns and cakes. First call was Peter Reid, Hope Street, then on to the "tin shop" and Skelton Street. If Peterhead F.C. had a home match we used to hurry, so that we could steal a peek over the wall at the sea end.

There were many football "heroes" in those days. "Middler" a keeper without peer, Harry Aitken and Billy Hutchison (I remember the day he had a broken leg) Petie Thomson - the rubber mannie - Sonny Hall, Chowie Imlah, Jimmy Campbell, Jock Low and many more.

Later came the McRobbies, Jim and Alex from the "Broch", Sodger Duthie and Jim Birnie (Broch), two of the finest half-backs I have ever seen! Johnnie "oor ba" Capoo and of course our own two local referees, Johnny Taylor and Peter Davidson (white inch).

Later still came the Dunraven team, nearly all of whom played senior for Peterhead - Alec Henderson, Bill Scott, Andrew Smith, Pattie Duncan, Billy Weir, Hector Bennett, my brother Jackie, Ayton Buchan, Joe Davidson, (his brother "Townie" was our trainer later on) and of course many must remember with gratitude Jimmy Reid the trainer and well know masseur! I remember him once bandaging my knee before a game, saying "You shouldna be playin fitba wi a knee like that." I simply said "Jimmy, if it wis you fit wid you dae?" Two words ended the conversation "Play" said Jimmy "Right" said I.

The junior league flourished with teams such as Dunraven, East End, Corinthians, Boddam, Academy F.P.'s, Buchanhaven Hearts and West End, and we had an annual game against Fraserburgh Junior League Select. I played for West End except for one season with Dunraven. West End was run by a Cameron, I think he was a painter. He lived in Love Lane, and our President was Baillie Christie, Ally Christie's grandfather. After one season with Dunraven I turned senior.

In one junior game, played in a howling gale, K.O. Smith kicked the ball right from one end past the opposing goal, and from the ground - a dead ball! I can only remember a few of the juniors of that league in addition to those I have already mentioned, Jimmy Lamb and, "Bapper" Ewan among them. "Bapper" came to Inverurie where he became a successful business man, and a loyal supporter of Inverurie Locos.

KIRK SOIREES AND "CLARKIES"

Earlier I mentioned "Clarkies" or to give it its more imposing title "The Palace Theatre", once a skating rink, then cinema-come-theatre. Clarkie always greeted his patrons with an entire resume of the programme. If the film billed did not turn up, he always seemed to have limitless supply of comedies, especially Charlie Chaplins which he would substitute. There I can remember seeing Charlie and Jackie Coogan in the Kid. I do remember there were a great many wet hankies.

What a mixture of tears and laughter the great master Charlie could produce and what a tonic it was, in a world which had so much poverty and sorrow - for an hour at least the world outside was forgotten.

It was there I saw "Bummer Gray" and his amateur Dramatic company in many fine plays such as "Peg of My Heart" etc. Johnny Buchan, "Middy" Mr. and Mrs. Gray, Donald Sutherland and Meg Connon. I think they put on a play annually.

Speaking of plays, there was another Dramatic company in Peterhead. They performed in the Rescue Hall (were they Reccabites?) I remember crying my eyes out one evening watching that old Drama "Tifty's Annie." I think one of my father's bakers was the trumpeter.

I can also remember the "Muckle Kirk" soiree, an annual event attended by a packed audience in the Rescue Hall. The Sunday School classes put on little items, plays, skits etc. My first appearance was in a skit. Dressed in a tail coat and long trousers, I was supposed to be a Doctor. I was petrified. I doubt if anyone in the audience heard one word I uttered - if indeed I did utter? The soiree was a great occasion. The whole family went, and teas and buns were provided. There were no tables, the tea and buns were consumed in your seats. Mention of Sunday school brings a must, Mrs. Forest, whose husband was manager of the Dundee Equitable, in Queen Street, and whose son was Dr. Alisdair Forest (her daughter Marion I mentioned in a school episode). She gave up a tremendous amount of her time to young folks! In the winter evenings, her house in Cairntrodlie would be crammed with Sunday school pupils being prepared for exams and boy scouts being instructed in basketry etc. preparing for badges.

AND SCHOOLBOY TRICKS!

Many of us must have very many happy memories of Peterhead Academy! - the old saying is really true for most people - "Your happiest days are your school-days!" When I think of some of the pranks we got up to - of how we must have tormented some of our teachers, "Old Bill" for example. We were really very fond of him, but he was so absent minded I doubt if he knew anything at all about what we were up to most of the time!

At one time, because of the "train pupils" having to leave by 3.30, we had to come back half an hour earlier after lunch, for Science classes. We came in at 1 o'clock instead of 1.30. "Old Bill" was involved in supervising at 1.30, so when the 1.30 bell went, one of the windows looking out to York Street was opened, and any late-comers came in there. The difference in numbers was never noticed! In one Science lab there was a trapdoor in the floor. On one occasion "Old Bill" left the room at 1.30 and two or three boys went down through the trapdoor. A stool was placed over the trapdoor and someone sat on it. "Old Bill" came in, taught a lesson and went out again, giving us instructions to get on with our writing up. The trap-door was opened up, and the boys came up again. There absence was never noticed!

On another occasion a boy was being "ducked!" It was his birthday (I think it was K. O. Smith). When "Old Bill" went out K. O. was grabbed and pulled to the sink nearest the door. He struggled and held onto the treble tap arrangement. Suddenly the whole contraption snapped off altogether., and a stream of water flew in the direction of the door. It could not have been timed better (or worse) because just at that moment the door opened, and Mr. Rice and "Old Bill" were drenched!

We had a new music teacher, a male at that, Mr. Kimberley Smith, I remember, a fine big speciman of a man he was. His wife was a trained Opera singer, and, one afternoon, the girls were invited to go to the music room after school, and she was to entertain them. We boys were "huffed" that we were not asked, and when the entertainment started, we were standing in a group in the Victoria Hall, possibly hoping we would get a last minute invitation, but no!, On a sudden impulse, I snatched the key from its hook and ran over, locked the music room door and replaced the key in the box at the foot of the sewing room stair. We all fled home! Mr. Rice was locked in with them! Next morning I was summoned to Mr. Rice's office. How he knew I do not know to this day but there were no questions asked, he knew. I'll say no more except to say that our music teacher, when I apologised, simply said "It is very easy Nicol, to kick even an elephant, when its back is turned". And from then on the whole incident was forgotten.

In time I was to see, and experience, the other side of the picture, from being the pupil, I was to become the teacher, but of that more anon.

WITH TOMMY MORGAN IN PETERHEAD PRISON!

From the sublime to the ridiculous! I first saw Tommy Morgan (Clairty!, Clairty!) in the Palace or to give it its better know name Clarkies! He spent a winter season in Peterhead with his company. They rehearsed and prepared their scenery in the Y.M.C.A. in Narrow Lane! His audience usually consisted of about 20 to 30 people - mostly lads from the Y.M.C..A. He used to make personal remarks and jokes about them, I remember especially "Watchie" Simmers (Gordon). I remember going with Tommy to H. M. Prison to entertain the convicts. This was quite an experience! We had to wait inside the outer gate for quite a while. Then an old bent figure of a man appeared carrying a set of bagpipes which he proceeded to tune up. Clad in his convict suit he played us across the courtyard and into the hall and down the centre aisle on to the platform!

I remember we had our hands in our pockets, because we had been warned that some of the inmates could steal the shirt off one's back! I can remember thinking "what a peculiar church, with so many pulpits!" Armed warders sat in pulpit-like boxes high-up in each corner. All the way down the aisle came whispers "Gies a fag mister!"

What a welcome we got! - and one of the corniest of gags in an opening skit, brought the house down. Tommy started to tell some gags, and his foil, (I forget his name) interrupted him by running across the stage in front of him, dressed as A little boy and carrying a pail and spade, "here youse, far d'ye think ye're gaun?" asked Tommy. Holding up his pail & spade he replied, "Ah'm awa tae Peterheed tae bail my brither oot!"

The singer in the group had quite a nice voice, and when he sang "Danny Boy" I don't think there was a dry eye in the whole audience! Some of the inmates broke down completely. The last time I saw Tommy was years later in the Tivoli in Aberdeen. He threw a rose to Meg Connon, who was sitting in the box overlooking the stage.

CRICKET AND CIGARS!

I have spoken about football at some length, but so far, I have not mentioned cricket. I suppose because we played very little cricket during my school days, and we certainly never had any school cricket. This was due to a great extent to the cold inclement weather in the Peterhead area, but Peterhead had its "Halcyon" days in cricket too!

Tom Gibb's father, who was a sawyer to trade, was an excellent bat. He passed his ability to Tom, but unfortunately Tom did not get much opportunity to exercise his talent. I can remember there was a very good cricket team which played at Aden, where the pitch was well sheltered. I can remember Bill Gibson getting his upper lip so badly split when fielding close in,that he wore a moustache from then on! I remember "Speed" Morrison's demoniacal expression when he raced up to hurl his fast bumpers down the wicket to a "Broch" opponent! His brother Ruthven was an excellent bat!

My other memory of cricket in the "Blue Toon" is quite a different one! For some time attempts were made to revive the game in Peterhead, by using a pitch in the Recreation Park (football';s hallowed ground!) One day I went up there to watch a game with my brother Jack. We were sitting in the old Pittodrie stand,and he produced, of all things, cigars which he had "pinched" from my father's stock. He proceeded to light one and handed it to me. I think I would have been about 9 or 10 years old at the time. After two or three puffs I was so ill that I spent the rest of the afternoon flat on my back on the grass, feeling very sick indeed!

PICNICS, TENNIS AND STRAWBERRIES

I spoke of Sunday school, and this of course brings memories of picnics! What fun the child of today misses! Picnic day usually meant transport by horse lorries, with forms tied back to back, so that half sat facing west and half facing east! - so to speak!

We would be driven out to Ravenscraig, and there we had an afternoon of races, hoopla, "Aunt Sally" and such-like amusements. Aunt Sally was a large wooden figure, with a clay pipe sticking in its mouth. One had to try to break the pipe by throwing wooden "batons" at it!

Water was boiled in a huge pot (usually a wash-house boiler), over an open fire, and everyone enjoyed a "Cuppa" despite the fact that it tasted strongly of smoke and it had been stirred with a "broom bush".

Some years later we went as far as Longside. On these occasions we went by "special train". When we were older we joined the "Bible class" and we would go the castle of Gight for our picnic.

As bible class members we were granted the use of a grass lawn tennis court at the manse one evening a week. Quite a crowd of us used to go there. Charlie and Ben Collie, Doddie Gibson, Jackie, Edith Reid, Bessie Robertson and Myra Dickie among others.

From tennis to strawberries - Peterhead strawberries were well known especially among the fisher folk from Yarmouth and Lowestoft! On a Saturday afternoon they would flock up to "Westies", just off Cairntrodlie and Grange Gardens. There is a school there now where once was a wonderful Market garden, completely sheltered by bushes, so that inside it was difficult to realise you were actually in Peterhead! There, in wooden chalets the fisher folk would partake of strawberries and cream. "Westie" sold all kinds of vegetables and fruit. He also sold these throughout the town from a horse "cartie!"

Nearby were two other strawberry farms. Strawberry Bank was one. They sold strawberries in "punnets", and, I was always intrigued by this, - gooseberries were sold by the pint! Mr. West was a very pleasant faced, weather-beaten gentleman, and he always had a few extra berries for the messenger.

THE "BLUE TOON", THE SEA AND SHIPWRECKS

No one can think of Peterhead without thinking of the sea, the calm beauty of its peaceful mood, and the magnificence of its raging angry moments. I have seen the waves break over the embankment and flood Charlotte Street. I have watched the life-boat being launched into seas which I felt certain would engulf her. I remember one dark winter night, with a howling, shrieking gale which was blowing salt spray right up Merchant Street. I stood shivering with a crowd, gathered to watch a launching. Comments among the fishermen experts standing there were "They'll never launch her in that". Then a thrill of excitement rippled through the gathering "She's away!" and sure enough through the wind one could here (or almost feel) the chug, chug of the life-boat's engines, and then on the crest of a wave, we caught a glimpse of her navigation lights before she dived once more into the depths of another trough. Someone in the crowd remarked "It's an Aberdein trawler, she's on the reef at Rattray. They'll nivir get near her wi the life-boat". Next morning the life-boat lay quietly in the South Harbour, and the trawler's crew lay snugly asleep in the "Deep Sea Mission". The life-boat was sailed right on board the wreck, and the crew jumped from the rigging. The next big wave washed the life-boat overboard again and she was on her way home. I remember, years later, trying that night's coxswain to tell me about that rescue. I can't remember if it was "Nape" or "Tatters" he was called, but, sitting there in the life-boat shed with his open bible before him, he would only repeat, "We only did fit hit tae be deen - Wi, God's help!"

My earliest recollection of a shipwreck was of a vessel named the "Tomtit". It was during World War one and the "Tomtit" was wrecked on that treacherous rock, the "Horse-back" near the harbour entrance. Due to a tragic mix-up in communications, the order was given to launch the life-boat. On her way down the slip-way, within a stones throw of the "Horse-back" she was overwhelmed by a vicious wave, which engulfed her, and smashed her off the slip-way. If I remember rightly all aboard were lost. The real tragedy was that the entire crew of the wreck were landed safely by the life-saving apparatus (by breeches bouy).

During my thirty years in Peterhead I was to learn that even Hitler's U-Boats, war-ships and bombers were childs' play compared to the fury of a really vicious storm at sea. Coxsawin McLean of the "Julia Park Barry of Glasgow" (the life-boat stationed at Peterhead during World War two) could certainly testify to that. In January 1942 a terrible hurricane accompanied by a blinding snowstorm hit North East Scotland. In three days, with its crew having little or no sleep, Cox McLean's life-boat had performed four rescue missions and had saved no less than one hundred and six lives. For this, Cox McLean was awarded the Gold Medal for conspicuous gallantry, his engineer, David Wiseman, the silver medal, and the rest of the crew bronze medals. All of them were, to the public eye, just plain ordinary fishermen modest and unassuming, and just doing their job.

Of the many shipwrecks off Peterhead a few come more rapidly to mind than others. During World War One, two coal boats were driven ashore in front of what is now the

"Lido" and Marina in the South Bay. For years after coal was gathered from the beach by the locals.

One shipwreck which I actually witnessed happened about mid-day one Christmas day. At this time the South Bay was protected by only one breakwater, the south one. As a result the bay was a death trap in a North-easter. Believe me this Christmas day we had a real "humdinger" of a North-easter. A trawler was dragging her anchor and this in spite of steaming ahead into the gale. A fishermen beside me said "his only chance is to swing round full steam ahead towards the rocks, and then swing round again into the bay". The trawl skipper performed this manoeuvre once successfully, but when he attempted to repeat it the unfortunate trawler was driven hard on to the rocks beneath the prison. By this time the coastguards had set up the rescue apparatus, and the entire crew were landed safely ashore.

Making my way home to roast turkey and "Plum-duff" I could really appreciate how lucky we land-lubbers were.

I can remember one spring day (it was during the highers) there had been a dense fog during the night and no less than three drifters had run aground. I went with a pal to the mouth of the Ugie and I photographed him. When the "snap" was printed, in it could be seen all three wrecks. One was on the reefs at Rattray, a second was on the rocks at Craigewan Head and the third was high and dry in the channel of the Ugie. It was called the "Firsby" (see photograph). Some of the crew of the one on Craigewan Head were drowned attempting to put out a "kedge" anchor. I remember some time later Bruce Findlay and I watched the remains of a body being recovered from the sands behind the eighth tee (at that time the cottage hole).

In September 1930 the entire North east coast line was enveloped in a dense fog. The "Ellerman" liner "City of Osaka" completely missed her course, and ran straight into a gully in the cliffs off Stirling Hill, Boddam. I often wonder how they missed hearing the "Buchan Coo" (the foghorn at Buchan Ness). My father and I went out to see the wreck next day, and it was unbelievable in fog-free daylight to see this vessel stranded in this way. The sight of it reminded me of the tale of the Boddamers and the Monkey. A shipwreck many years ago, brought the locals out in force. On board the wreck was a monkey and the story is that the poor creature was hanged by the superstitious locals who had never seen such a creature before.

Another wreck which I actually saw happen, was during World War two. Italy had just declared war, mistakenly thinking the fighting was all over. All Italian ships were ordered to neutral ports. If this was not possible then the vessel was to be scuttled. An Italian ship off Peterhead was boarded by a naval crew, after her captain had attempted to scuttle her. She had on board a valuable cargo, and a Peterhead pilot offered his services to steer her into Peterhead bay. The naval commander was not going to share his valuable "prize" with anyone so he refused help. I was standing on the North Harbour wall with an elderly fisherman. Pointing to some broken water, well out of the Italian ships course, he said to me "see that broken water there, that man disnae ken the currents here, he'll finish up on that reef there and she'll brak her back!" Sure enough, that is exactly what happened, and next day nothing could be seen of the vessel. The Italian "prize" and her valuable cargo were lost. The treacherous currents round the North Head at Peterhead have claimed many a victim. I rather like the story of the old fisherman whose boat was seen to be in trouble off the North Head. The life-boat was launched and when it came alongside the old man berated the Coxswain and said "Ye shid hae mair sense than come oot here in es kine o widder man!"

FOG AT MIDNIGHT!

Auld "Hornie's" oot the nicht for sure,
It's foggy, black, the witchin' oor,
Wi, ill intent he's oot for trouble,
So keep a look oot, caution double!
Foggy swirls, - a tree's a ghost,
Ae turnin, wrang, an ye are lost,
Warlocks, Bogles on yer mind,
Creepy, crawlies ivry kind,
Fingers crossed, step oot wi care,
Ae step wrang - it needs nae mair,
The Deil will grab ye, that's for sure,
An aince he grabs there's nae, nae cure,
Ye're his for good (or rather evil!)
An fa wints hoos room wi the Deevil?

The "Firsby" in the Ugie Channel

33

PERSONALITIES - POLITICAL AND OTHERWISE!

We used to sing "Vote, vote, vote for Freddy Martin!" or Wallace who was the blind "M.P.'s political opponent in several elections. "Vote! vote, vote for his names sake." In those days even the youngsters became excited at election time - although they had no idea what it was all about.

What about the annual dances and parties held in the Old Palace Hotel ballroom - or the dancing classes held there by Miss Mitchell (from Inverugie) - the old Palace Hotel ballroom - now a cocktail lounge. I came across an old photograph of a group of students, taken at a dance held at the end of "Students Week" the week when we toured the district collecting for Aberdeen Royal Infirmary. The charities collection had broken all records, and we were winding down, ready to return to normal life once again! The group includes many whose names I have forgotten, but among them were "Ali" Macintosh, Billy and Nancy Rice, Tony Wildgoose, Alec Cumming, Bill Birnie, Dorothy Hacket, "Chatty" Mair, Eva Buchan, Bill Rankine, the then Buchan Observer editor, Mr. Taylor's daughter, John Geddes, Eileen Gibson and John Cordinor (who became provost of Ellon). Looking at the photo I was surprised that David Steel is not in it. He was a classmate of ours - I think his father was the first C.O.O.P. manager in Peterhead. He was the minister of the church attached to Linlithgow Palace, and is now retired in Edinburgh. His son is Sir David Steel of political fame!

Another personality of my childhood days whom I ought to remember was "Worthy!" What the gentlemans real name was I have no idea. I can picture him yet, one arm missing, sitting up on the drivers seat of his lorry, horse of course, and sitting beside him, usually one or two of us youngsters. He had a way with children, as well as with horses. I remember well he taught us to makes whips which really cracked! - the thong or cracking part was whipcord. The boots and shoes in those days came by rail, and in wooden boxes so huge, that, behind Dunn's shop, in the post office close, in Thistle Street, was a pile of empties used as "housies" and castles - an ideal playground for "kids!"

Personalities - memory plays funny tricks at times, and I have no doubt I have forgotten many noteworthy people. How could I ever forget Baillie Booth of Downiehills? His kenspeckle figure - he was a magnificent figure of a man and his very own tweed suits made him recognisable streets away! Linked with him must be the name of Boothby! It was Baillie Booth who first recognised the genius budding in that raw, young politician he first spotted at an Orkney, (or was it Shetland?) cattle sale. I have many happy memories of Bob Boothby, and also of Lord Boothby, although he would not even recognise my name, since we never met! Most of the memories are of the pleasures of listening to his witty, sparkling repartee delivered in that deep, fruity voice, but two of them are slightly different!

I remember early one morning, standing outside my father's shop in Marischal Street. I was looking down the street, wondering what on earth that dreadful noise was. Up the street came a filthy, dirty car. One of the front tyres was punctured and it was in tatters. The noise was the wheel rim "clattering" on the road and the rattling caused by this, throughout the whole body of the car! Grasping the wheel, eyes red rimmed, obviously long on the road, and sleepless, there sat the character I knew as Bob Boothby! He had driven all night and had not even stopped to change wheels. He was probably on a business visit to his great friend - the fishermen's leader, Tom Buchan! The other memory of Boothby concerns one of his first meetings in Peterhead, in the Rescue Hall. Fred Martin - the blind M.P. had held East Aberdeenshire for some time and now during the years of depression, a strong Socialist element was appearing in Peterhead. The Rescue Hall was packed to the door, and many of the audience were determined that this young "so and so" was not going to get a hearing! He was going to get such a "heckling" that he would not forget Peterhead in a hurry! Within minutes he had them "eating out of his hand", and laughing at his witty handling of the hecklers! He had a genius for feeling out the pulse of a meeting, and he was at his best when being "heckled strongly!" A man of his calibre is sorely needed in the North East today - perhaps he could sort out the "oil situation" just as he sorted out the fishing problems in his hey day!

THE GREAT PICTURE HOUSE FIRE AND "EMPRESS HALL!"

Jumping a few years more, I spoke earlier of "Aubreys" the picture house. Underneath it and extending right back to Tolbooth Wynd was built a magnificent Dance Hall with an excellent suite of ante-rooms "The Empress Hall!" The manager of the picture house at the time was Leander Wilkinson. He formed a dance band in which he played drums and also did the vocals. He was quite good too!

Then Jim Massie - Daves elder brother, started a dance band amongst the Y.M.C.A. boys. He was a self taught pianist, and although he played entirely by ear, he was very good! He told me that once the band was established, if he could find a real pianist (as he put it), one who could read music, he would withdraw. When "Tyre Johnny" appeared, Jimmy did retire. The band became one of the best known in the district!

Piano - "Tyre Johnnie" - Drums and Vocals Dave Massie - Bass Fiddle Bill Colvin - Banjo/Mandolin Jimmy Masson - I forget the rest, but my two brothers Jim and Ernest later played tenor and alto saxaphones.

One night my father wakened me and asked me to come with him. The police had telephoned him to come down town urgently. The Empress Hall was on fire and his property was in danger. What a sight met our eyes when we reached Marischal Street. The whole top half of the street was ablaze! The first thing I noticed was a fireman standing, one foot on the pavement in front of Bill Leslie's shop (now Hepworths) directing his hose towards the fire. The trickle of water from his hose was not even reaching the window! All the fire hoses were rotten, and jets of water were spurting from them all the way up the street! The water, instead of dowsing the fire was washing down Marischal Street!

Had not a detachment of Aberdeen Fire Brigade arrived in double quick time, the fire would have swept right down the whole length of Marischal Street! Quickly firemen raced up ladders on to the roof of the house next to "Fyffe and Duncans" shop and breaking through with axes soon had part of the fire under control! Water was pumped up Broad Street from the harbour, and also from the "Bogie Hole" up Merchant Street! All at once there was a tremendous explosion skywards. In the Picture House, apparently there had been a stock of old films, and the fire had reached them! Curiously enough, Simpson the Chemists shop and store rooms were never reached otherwise the old Town House would have been destroyed.

What a scene of destruction was left! The dance hall was never re-built nor was the Picture House! With the Empress Hall went the memories of dancing, rotating mirrors reflecting coloured lights around the ballroom, roller-skating, crazy golf and of course the Senior Citizens annual Christmas treat! The loss of the hall left a blank in the social life of Peterhead which was never filled I suppose, until Mr. and Mrs. Stevenson built the hall adjoining the Palace Hotel.

SMUGGLERS AND TUNNELS!

Peterhead had its tales of smugglers, caves and tunnels, but I must say I never heard of a Peterhead ghost! The "Angel of Mons" yes, but never a ghost!

We had an old "pub" in the Longate which was reputed to have been the haunt of the smugglers of Rattray! We had the deep, black dungeon in the backyard in Prince Street next to the "Brethern" Hall, near Thistle Street. No one seemed to know where it ended, but it was reputed to end in a tunnel!

One interesting tunnel was discovered while Arbuthnot House was being converted to Town Offices! Alex Reid, a joiner with John May, the expert who taught my brother Jackie his trade, was on this job with Jackie. They came on a door in the cellars, which, being curious, they forced open! They found a tunnel which they followed quite a distance up Broad Street. There it was completely blocked up by a "cave in!" The Arbuthnot House end was sealed off so I doubt if we will ever discover where it went. In this connection I received a very surprising letter from a Peterhead exile living in the U.S.A. This lady had lived in one of the lodges at Dales House and remembered being taken to Dales House and being shown a trapdoor which, she was told was the entrance to a tunnel leading to ARBUTHNOT HOUSE! She enclosed a sketch showing the room and the exact position of the trapdoor! Who knows!

Down near the harbour we had, at the foot of Merchant Street, the "Hallelujah Lobby!" How it ever got this name I have no idea, but in my young days it was a "Model Lodging House." Once upon a time, when Peterhead was a Royal Spa! I imagine it must have been a magnificent mansion, situated right opposite the "Mineral Well and Baths." This well unfortunately stopped producing, and has now been obliterated! (and the baths have also disappeared!) The other mineral spring is at the Gadle Braes, not far from the coast-guard station. I remember once sampling the water there with some visitors, and their description of the taste is unprintable - but, of course, in the old days, it was believed the worse the taste - the better a medicine was for you!

FISHING, DOOKING AND A TRIP IN THE LIFE-BOAT!

My brother Jackie and his wife spent a weekend with us at Easter and we visited my sister Eva and her husband Robbie Stephen in Aberdeen. We had a real good "natter" about old times. I discovered that Dame Clara Butt's visit to Peterhead was not to give concerts to the wounded, but to raise money in aid of the Red Cross!

Jackie was two years my elder and so was given the unenviable job of looking after his little brother, and what a devil for mischief he was. We were dared to go near the embankment (it was a favourite fishing spot) so we went fishing regularly off the embankment! We caught mostly "geats" and "podlies" but we also caught an occasional cod (usually small and of the "warry" codling variety) and quite often a "gundy." When the fish were not "hosin," (biting) we would use a whole herring and catch crabs!

Sometimes, if the weather was pleasant, we would strip off and go dookin off the rocks at the end of the embankment! Speaking of what we caught, we quite often caught a good hiding when we came home stinking of fish! So many boys fell into the harbour that we were dared to go there (unless accompanied by an adult.) The result was Jackie and I often went to the harbour as well! One such occasion was on a life-boat week Saturday. The life-boat was making trips round the Skerry Rock at a "bob" a time. Jack was always a great opportunist, and so there we were standing close to the Harbour's edge, watching a crowd disembark from the lifeboat. (I remember the tide was out and I was looking down on to the bows of the boat with Jackie behind me holding my waist.) There was a shout from the "Cox", "Last trip - no charge!" and before he had finished speaking, I was lying flat across the white bows and Jackie was sprawling on top of me. I don't know to this day whether he pushed me, or the crowd pressure pushed us both, but I have my suspicions!

We both enjoyed the trip enormously, (although I was a bit worried about Mother finding out) until just before entering the harbour, I succumbed to temptation, and this was my downfall! Two little girls, close neighbours of ours, whose names shall not be mentioned, had been violently sick, and I had religiously kept my eyes, and my mind on other things, until we were swinging round to pass the "Horse-back" and enter the harbour. Then, one fatal glance, my stomach heaved, and I gasped "Jackie, I'm going to be sick!" "Not on me you're not!" and he grabbed me and stuck my head over the side. I remember staggering up Broad Street, dodging the Town House spire, which kept swinging down to bash me on the head - and - I remember my mother's look when she saw my condition. Fortunately she thought I had suffered enough. I agreed with her, and no more was said!

Jackie was not only an opportunist, but very resourceful as well! I remember one night, years later, he was stranded in the semi-dark, and miles from home with a puncture (motor-bike.) He had no repair outfit, not even a pump, but he was determined to get home - and - he was not going to walk! Nor was he going to damage the tyre. He levered the tyre partly off, and stuffed it with grass! He got home, slowly, uncomfortably, but safely - and - his tyre was undamaged!

Jackie was also, in some ways, unlucky - being a young devil, he was always up to some mischief, and was always apt to be blamed, whether guilty or not! After my motor-cycle accident, which practically said finish to my playing football, he was blamed for allowing me to have his bike, although he did not even know I had it!

When I had recovered I played in two trial games before Peterhead played Vale of Leven (I think it was a third round Scottish tie.) Jackie crossed the ball about 6 or 8 yards out and and about 3 feet off the ground. I dived horizontally to cut out the cross, and was kicked between the shoulder-blades, I dropped, completely paralysed, and as I fell I was kicked on the head. Jackie, who had followed up his cross, turned a somersault over me, and finished up suspended by his feet in the back of the net. I only discovered during this last visit, that he was severely ticked off for nearly killing me, although the truth was, he nearly broke his neck trying to avoid me!

"SANDIKIE ROBERTSON, BOWLS AND STRAWBERRIES & ICE CREAM!"

Thinking of the Palace Hotel reminds me of my Central School days. We often played, after school in the yard behind the Palace. There were the stables and horses, and of course, the pigs. The pig sty in the corner was a great source of interest. We used to marvel that the pigs could even live in such filth, besides eat and sleep there! Above the pig sty was a work-shop. I forget the gentleman's name who worked there, but I do remember he was a cripple - crippled in his legs and his feet - but well compensated by the gift of an unusually skilled pair of hands! He used to get butter (or lard) barrels from my father (I think they were Russian and made of oak!) From these he used to fashion handsome cabinets and tables. We had one which held gramophone records and another which was a smokers cabinet. It had drawers for cigarettes and tobacco, and it had a neat pipe-rack built in to it.

Up in St. Mary Street lived another gentleman who had also a skilled pair of hands. In his case, however, he had in addition the gift of imparting his skill to others. Many a young man, about to be married, made the most of his furniture under the skilled tuition of Mr. Robertson - affectionately known as "Sandikie" to almost everyone - "Shokio" to a few. This was a name given to him by some senior boys. Sandikie always wore a hard collar, called a choker, and this was their fun translation into "french" chokier hence Shokio!

Manual instructor at the Academy, his evening classes were so popular that for some time, he even held classes on Saturdays! His end of term exhibitions were eye-openers, with a magnificent display of furniture of all kinds, carved or plain! He had a house out at Rora, with a huge garden, in which, among other things, he grew a great quantity of strawberries. The house was a thatched cottage, the only one left in the district. My wife's eldest sister, Janet, and her husband Bill Strachan, the Rora blacksmith, lived next door so we were frequent visitors. Sandikie bought one of Sutherland's double deckers which was set up, on blocks, at the foot of the garden, and was converted into a neat little house, with a kitchen, sitting room and bedroom! Years later, when my wife and I moved in from the Blackhouse bungalow to the flat in St. Mary Street, Mr. and Mrs Robertson lived in the flat below us. We found them the best neighbours. Their son Steve who was a schoolmate of mine, was a solicitor in Aberdeen.

Another game from which I have fond memory is bowls, not competitive in the real sense, but certainly competitive in the fun sense. Happy Buchan, John Geddes, Bill Baird and I used to play challenge games against rinks of O.A.P.'s and fishermen regularly at the Public Green during the summer and on the indoor rinks above the Masonic Temple during the winter. This was during my student days - student days over, I was to return to Peterhead as a teacher and in a school, which I must admit until then, I scarcely knew existed - Peterhead North!

Strawberries - cream - Ice-cream!!! Peterhead has always been famous for its ice-cream. We had Guilianotti in Marischal Street (later Marioni's) Ucelloti, opposite the "Muckle Kirk", Ferrari in Rose Street, Bicocci and Zanre in Queen Street, Becci in Back-gate among others. Chips and ice-cream do not go well together, but in Peterhead, at any rate they did go well together.

In Peterhead the best of each was produced by Italians, with one exception. Pow's Chay was the only one I ever knew who could make ice-cream equal in quality to the Italians. He opened a shop in King Street, after selling his ice-cream from a bicycle propelled barrow!

Some of the ice-cream shops had billiard saloons as well. Louis Ucelloti had two tables upstairs behind his shop, and this was for some time the favourite haunt of a few of us. There was "Curly" Smith, Jimmy Donald (sergeant Donald's son), "Cody" Alex Cordiner, Bobby Collie, Dave Cordiner and several others. We had some tussles, and I can remember one evening, when Dave was in cracking form, we finished a frame of snooker in less than ten minutes. When Marioni's built their new saloon we played there. Louis Marioni was an expert players. Many times I played him 100 up and usually only had one visit to the table!

PETERHEAD'S EVER CHANGING FACE!

Peterhead in the thirties was a vastly different place from the Peterhead we know now! When we look around us now, and when we talk of the permissive society, I often think back to the "Blue Toon" I knew. It was the very opposite of permissive! On Saturday evenings all the children's swings and chutes etc. were padlocked so that they could not be used on the "Sabbath." I often shake my head and wonder if I only dreamed this, but alas it was only too true! Provost Schultz used to make what became known as his annual plea - a motion that the children's playgrounds, swings, chutes etc. should not be padlocked but should be open for use, and also that tea rooms in the town should be allowed to open on Sundays if they wished! I well remember his surprise when eventually he got his way. I can well remember the "scandalous behaviour" of many of our young folks when they were going to the "Lido" to bathe when, according to their betters, they ought to have been going to Church! The Lido at this time consisted of a tiny strip of sand, bounded at the north end by a filthy dirty sewage outlet below the old Brickworks, and at the south end by the rocks immediately below the Prison Governor's house. An old boat lay on its side on the sands and we sometimes undressed behind it!

Sundays previously to this emancipation consisted of a long walk, in the afternoon out the "Broch" road by the "Chyne" bridge, round Howe of Buchan and home by the west road - or up by "Geordie Murray's" roadie and on to the Cruives (or Pinkie Braes) at Inverugie. A favourite stop on a hot Sunday afternoon was at "Muggie Black's" farm where we could get a foaming, cream topped glass of fresh milk for one old penny (quite often for nothing!) Alas even "Muggie's" farm is no longer there. If we felt lazy, we might just go "ower the water" and walk the "bents", or play on the old boats in the creek below the first tee! Perhaps, if it was really sunny, we would just lie on the sands. We, in this case were a group of "Pals" including, Dave Massie, "Curly" Smith, Doddy Forest, "Barry" Brown, Jimmy Donald, "Cody" (Alex) Cordiner.

Mention of the Cruives reminds me of the Inverugie Tennis Club and the tennis courts above. When I was a boy, it had been a very active club, and produced such stars as the Mitchell family, Johnny R.L. (Bobby) and the rest of them. A slightly older generation than mine played there, and used the old mill for dances, in the summer evenings. Mention of "Muggie" Black - I can see her yet in her milk cart with its shining milk cans and its sparkling clean measures, 1/2 pint, 1 pint and quart - I can still hear her horsie clop-clop down Queen Street and along Marischal Street. There were quite a number of these milk-carts or "floats" on the streets in these days, among them Robertsons (Blackhills), Mckays (Grange), Petries from Kirk Street, one from Waterside, Lambs from Cowesrieve and also from Tortorston, and many others! I remember when I came home for holidays Mr. Robertson always said to mother "Well the calfie's hame again!"

THE YESTER YEARS

Whilst writing these reminiscences of my childhood in Peterhead, memories have come flooding back - disjointed, I agree, but many of them as vivid as if only yesterday. Where have all the "characters" gone? I mentioned that eminent figure of Mr. C. D. Rice striding down York Street to lunch, his black coat tails swinging behind him in the snell sea breeze. In St. Peter Street another such figure was often to be seen, but he carried his "black bag". This was Dr. Smith who's son K. O. Smith used to play in goal for the F.P.'s football team. Outside the big house at the corner of Queen Street and King Street stood a beautiful Rolls Royce, resplendent with chauffeur in spotless uniform. I can see the Rolls yet, every square centimetre of it shining like a mirror. Down the steps from the house would come that immaculately dressed, burly figure, Dr. Gillespie, off to visit his patients.

Then there was Mr. Clark, who seemed to have cigars that lasted for ever. Whether he was behind his shop counter in Marischal Street or at the door of his cinema (Clarkies in Hanover Street) always the cigar puffed away.

At the other end of the town was Aubreys (The Picture House), and there during matinees, the children were controlled by Mr. Mennie, who wielded a long bamboo cane, like a fishing rod. With this he could and did whack a noisy child, even if he or she sat in a centre seat.

Eddie Lumsden, the shoemaker, Ritchie the blacksmith (Smiddy Ritchie), Whyte the saddler, all made us welcome in their workshops, and many's the hour I spent stitching football covers with rositie ends, or pumping the smiddy bellows whilst Mr. Ritchie fashioned a gird and cleek or sledge runners for me. Then no one could forget "Cassies" where despite the unprepossessing window display, one could buy the finest and juiciest "Locust beans" and the very best from a large selection of the finest teas and coffees. Many's the pound of "broken Pekoe or Orange Pekoe" I was sent to buy there. Or who can forget "Retties" grocer shop in the Kirk Toon where, outside the door, hung a display of large "hard fish" (dried cod).

I often think of our favourite playground, Prince Street, between Thistle Street and the Palace Hotel. Street football, with jackets for goalposts, or that great favourite "Saps and Soldiers" were played there. The great advantage was the numerous escape routes. When the cry A.B.C.R.L. (a bobby coming run lads) rang out, you could either shin over into Connons yard and over the inner wall and out into Albion Street, or one could bolt through the Palace Yard to St. Peter Street, or one could even disappear into Simpson's cartwright yard or into the foundry. I don't think the bobbies every really tried to catch us for, apart from the risk of breaking a window, with only horse traffic, we were really doing no harm.

Mention of Connon's yard brings back memories of the horse buses. Each hotel had one - a small bus drawn by a horse, which met each train and transported travellers and baggage to their respective hotels. Mr. Connon drove one of these. Then we had a large horse drawn bus (Bob Reids) which ran to Boddam. A special treat in the summer was a run to Boddam on this bus and a picnic on the rocks beneath the lighthouse.

Another favourite picnic spot was 'ower the watter!' This meant crossing the Ugie in a flat bottomed boat (cobble), which had a cable running through through rollers at each end. The cable was firmly fixed high up on each bank, and all you had to do was to stand up in the cobble and pull on the cable. This propelled the boat "ower the watter!" I think the charge was one penny and a "maik" (halfpenny) for children. The golden sands and the magnificent "bents" were a great attraction and when you were young, the sun always shone of course all summer.

Every town and village, in the old days, as well as its characters, had its "worthies". Peterhead was no exception, and I can remember quite a few. "Curly Wurly", who sat on the "Muckle Kirk" dyke a great deal, with his cronies (when they were not walking the gutters picking up "tabbies", cigarette ends). When we shouted "Curly Wurly" he duly obliged, and growling and scowling, he would chase us, or pretend to. "Newly Come Over" - the town crier, was another. I never could make out what he was shouting, but his ringing bell always drew attention. For years I puzzled over his name, and then I heard he had emigrated to America, and soon after he returned to tell everyone he had newly come over (the Atlantic) and so he was named "Newly Come Over" and that was it.

Cecil Bannerman was a harmless soul who wheeled a barrow laden with bundles of kindlings - selling them for the "Poors House" in King Street.

Then there were the Street gangs which were common in the 1920's. There was great rivalry between the "Queenie Arabs", the "Buchaneers", the "Hillockers", the "Lovelaners", the "Langaters" and the "Kirktooners". Many a bloody battle took place between the rival gangs (I suspect more noise than blood). I remember vividly the "Warry Tangles" used by the Buchaneers against the Scouts when our hut was in Wilson Street. Most Friday nights we had to run the gauntlet of the Buchaneers to get home from the Scouts. The Scouts - more memories still of "Middy", Johnny Buchan, Mutt and Jeff - the Scout band - the Scout camps at Blackhills.

"Warry tangles!" These were long thick strands of sea-weed sometimes two or three inches thick and several feet long! Quite a fearsome weapon!

Talking about street football reminds me of an amusing incident - amusing looking back, but not so amusing at the time!

In front of the old town-house in Broad Street stands a statue of Field Marshal Keith, nearby is the police station. One day a group of boys had the temerity to play street football in Broad Street. Of course the inevitable happened - a policeman appeared. He succeeded in catching one of the boys and proceeded to ask him his name. "Marshall Keith" said the boy. The "bobby" gave him a resounding "clap on the lug" saying, "enough of your impudence my lad, your name and no nonsense!". The boys name really was Marshall Keith, so you can imagine the "bobbies" embarrassment!

GOLF, SWIMMING AND HOME LIFE ABOVE "PIE RENNIE'S!"

I have spoken more than once about George Beddie, who was an assistant at the Central School. George had been severely wounded in World War One! Very few people knew this since George never spoke of it. He was extremely fond of young people and devoted much of his spare time to children. On the golf course he was an excellent coach. He was not a long hitter, but more than made up for this by his great accuracy. He used to demonstrate how unnecessary it was to under-club! I remember once at the old eighth hole "The Cottage!" I had tried to "belt" an eight iron on to the green against a head wind and had, of course tailed it off into the little bunker on the right. George took a "Baffie" (equivalent I think to a three wood) and proceeded to play a nice easy shot up to the pin. This was when he showed me his wrist. It had been very badly shot up and as he explained he had per force to cultivate a nice easy swing!

George was also very interested in swimming, and he was so unselfish! Where many people would have "hogged" the "kudos", George preferred to work quietly in the background. He drew me into his arranging of school galas, and from the start treated me as if I were well experienced in the work, and not a raw beginner!

At the North School we had been plugging away at the education committee and at last we succeeded in getting the use of the swimming pool one afternoon a week (wednesday). One Wednesday the boys would go, and the next the girls. Such a thing as mixed bathing had not even been thought of (Heaven forbid!) I remember Miss Barclay and Miss Collie took the girls. Walter Stephen, (who later went to Kingswells as Headmaster) took half the boys from two till three, and I took the rest of them from four till five! It was such a pleasure to take these boys, I did not even envy Walter because he went during school hours and I went in my own time! We had great fun at these swimming sessions, and we held many successful galas. My father was disappointed to learn that the boys had a cup for competition whilst the girls had none, so he presented a cup for competitions among the girls.

In 1973 whilst Headmaster at Port Elphinstone, I was allowed HALF AN HOUR per week and only for ten weeks during the year. In addition, I was only allowed a maximum of 24 children. In the old days Walter and I took about 40 to 50 boys each for at least an hour! When we are all in the water the pool looked like a pond so full of tadpoles that it was difficult to find a place to dive in! The rings hanging from the roof beams were great fun too and helped to cultivate a rhythmic swing in addition to developing arm, shoulder and stomach muscles!

I remember Hector Bennett used to dive in from the gallery rail and retrieve coins for visitors! The bathmaster's thermometer must have been a very special one (sorry Mr. Falconer, not your fault I know!) It used to read temperatures of 80 or 82 degrees when I am perfectly certain the real temperature was nearer 40 to 45 degrees! After five minutes your teeth were chattering! In our modern pool at Inverurie, the water is so warm and comfortable, that one could stay in the water for hours! This makes it so much easier to teach children to swim. In the old days, to misquote "If a thing is worth doing it had to be the hard way!"

Memories of Peterhead - home life, schooldays, pleasures, chums, adult life, child-hood at home! Of early days my memories are very dim - of the "Places" behind the shop (Pie Rennies) where, on marble topped tables, fishermen were refreshed with pie and stone ginger (Ginger beer in stone bottles) memory is very dim indeed. Slightly clearer is the memory of the tea room above the shop - filled with sailors, soldiers and airmen from Lenabo, having tea or coffee and a cigarette. Memories of these wonderful cigarette cards, sets of which they helped us to collect!

In the shop itself, were Miss Burnett, Mary Elsie Beddie, Katie McKay, Nellie Whitecross, Nellie Yule and of course Mary Robertson. Home itself? Many, many happy memories! Winter evenings round the piano, or with the gramophone going (an H.M.V. which required winding.) Of evenings playing Ping Pong (now table tennis) on our dining table. It was oval and had bevelled edges, but this only added to the fun - evenings playing "Happy Families" or "Snap", Mothers chair at one side of the fire and Dads at the other, and every spare minute Mother sewing, darning and patching! When I think back, we boys were very hard on our clothes!

Through in the loft, above the shop, hanging from the "couples" (rafters) a trapeze, home made of course, with ropes and a broom handle. I remember the day it broke when I was suspended upside down it. I landed solidly on the top of my head on the floor. Neither the floor nor my head was seriously damaged, sound tribute to the workmanship of the builders and to the hard-headedness of the Scots!

I remember the arrival of that wonder - the wireless! We had a speaking tube from the kitchen to the shop. It had a whistle stopper at each end, so that by blowing, you could let someone know you had a message! We even had a telephone which could send messages through a wire - but always through the telephone exchange across the road, in the Post Office.

BUT NOW, WONDER OF WONDERS, we were making a machine called a crystal set, which would let us hear someone talking in London. There was the crystal with the magic cats-whisker. There were coils of copper wire wound round cardboard discs (in the way fishers wind their casts.) Some had 20 turns of wire, some 50, and some 100 and so on! There were intriguing things called ear-phones, which clipped over ones head with one "phone" tight over each ear! It was unbelievable!

When Scotlands footballers were playing Englands best at Hampden or Wembley we could listen to a man who was actually sitting watching the game. In the Radio Times was a diagram of the pitch squared off into eight squares. Next to the commentator sat a man who simply said "Square one or five or eight" and in ones mind one could almost see the play! I'll never forget the thrill of listening! We knew everything about the players, except perhaps what they had for lunch that day. I can still see it all and hear it. Allison or Chapman were the favourite commentators, and we would split up the earphones so that twice as many could listen!

Then came the day when my brother-and-law the late Robbie Stephen, assembled a new set for us. This was a grand wireless set. It had a loud speaker, horn shaped, which sat on top. Reception was still pretty dicey so everyone had to very quiet, especially at news time! That was one time we scarcely dared to breathe. It was an understood thing that news time was a time of silence. It was never asked, it was just understood, a mark I suppose of that now lost spirit of respect for parents and their wishes!

FIRES, EXPLOSIONS AND OTHER THINGS!

I spoke about the tremendous fire which burnt out Aubreys and the Empress Hall. I can remember quite vividly several other fires. Few of my generation could forget the fire which burned out the old Academy. How it started, I do not know. What I remember is how a few hundred pupils dreams of a long holiday were shattered when the old school in St. Peter Street (opposite Jimmy Sutherlands) was patched up. A few rough extensions were made, and lo and behold, school carried on, not quite as usual, but well enough. I remember the Science department was there, and "Micky" Mitchell was my science teacher. His favourite trick was to grab your hair and apply the meter stick. This was never done savagely, and to the best of my knowledge, was never resented. Mr. Mitchell went to Drumblade, and then to Fyvie as Headmaster in each case.

Another big fire I remember was Gavin's stables. This was opposite the wool-mill on the old road down to the embankment. The stables were destroyed, although I think most of the horses were saved, but it was a fearsome blaze. I can still recall the horrible smell of burning herring nets. There were quite often fires starting in kippering kilns. and herring net lofts. One such fire I recall was in Wilson Street. The stench of burning nets permeated the whole town, and the ruins smouldered for a long time. The fire station was in Windmill Street and was it a Mr. Wilcox or Mr. Mckay who was firemaster? The sight of the fire engine racing up the street is another vivid memory. It was pulled by horses, and the driver would be urging them on at great speed. One of the firemen was ringing the bell, a warning to clear the streets, and at the back another, a fireman in more senses than one, was busy stoking up the fire under the huge boiler making sure of a good head of steam to work the pump!

And now to explosions - during my life in Peterhead we had more than enough of these, mainly bombs dropped during the war, but two earlier ones were quite different! The town was rocked one day by a loud bang which had everyone jumping out of their skins. We soon learned there had been a dreadful accident down near the harbour. A Mr. McRobbie had been at work inside a ship's boiler when something had gone dreadfully wrong! An accumulation of gas inside the boiler had exploded and the unfortunate Mr. McRobbie had been killed!

The other explosion had a much happier ending, although it might have ended in a number of deaths. In our house above the shop in Marischal Street, a strong smell of gas was detected one day. The plumber arrived (obviously I shall not name him) but I can say he had years of experience behind him. The smell was strongest on the top floor in a passage which ran the length of the house. Our plumber proceeded to remove the skirting board. Obviously the space left was too small to allow him to put his head in to look at the pipe. The space was also very dark, and believe it or not the plumber proceeded to do exactly what "Charlie Chaplin" would have done. Yes - he lit a match and stuck it in the opening! A tremendous explosion followed immediately, but fortunately the accumulation of gas was in the middle floor of the house, and the explosion went downwards. The whole inner wall of the middle floor was blown to smithereens. Fortunately no-one was there at the time, I think we were all looking over the plumber's shoulder. The plumber and his mate, and Jackie and I were completely unhurt although shocked. I hate to think what could have happened if the leak had been lower still on the ground floor. There could have been seven or eight shop assistants there apart from any customers who could have been in the shop!

FROM PUPIL UNDER MR. RICE TO TEACHING IN
THE NORTH SCHOOL!

I spoke earlier of Mr. Rice being a true gentleman. At the same time he could be very severe, and we all preferred a strapping to a "telling off!" Madame and her peculiar Victorian ideas, I have also spoken of. She even considered it a sin for boys and girls to be seen talking together, and we were well warned about it! Young people do not resent authority, they do not even resent discipline - provided it's fair and provided they can understand the reason for it! - But authority wrongly used even although in "Madame's" case she was firmly convinced she was right, just makes young folk defiant and so, at lunch times groups of boys and girls could be seen chatting on the pavement in York Street outside the main gate of the school. Young folk today cannot believe that there used to be a high wall or fence separating the boy's playground from that of the girls!

One afternoon a group of boys, all fifth year pupils, were summoned to the Rector's office. I think there were about six or seven of us. I do recall Mr. Rice had a twinkle in his eyes which no amount of coughing could hide. "row boys" said he "Miss Mitchell has reported you to me for talking to girls. I know you will understand, I must take action to support my staff, and I know you will take this in the right spirit" or words to that effect! We lined up and held up one hand each. Mr. Rice, with a mischevious twinkle in his eyes, passed along the line tapping each upraised hand gently with his strap. At the e nd of the line, he paused, smiled, and opening his office door, ushered us out with this remark. "Now boys, you may inform Miss Mitchell I have dealt with you!" I often wonder what Miss Mitchell would think if she were to re-visit the Academy now? I met her many years later in Stonehaven. She was charming!

From pupil to teacher - As a student I always kept up my interest in school football and frequently refereed school games on a Saturday morning at the "Barclay" park. When I was appointed Science master at the "North" I found this experience invaluable. On my appointment to the "Ragged School" I was given a lot of good advice! I remember one thing that was impressed on me. "First thing you must do is buy a

46

"Lochgelly" (a special strap) they're a tough bunch there at the North! Let me state here and now, that far from being a tough bunch, they were as nice a bunch of "kids" as it has been my pleasure and privilege to teach! All they required was to be treated like human beings and they responded. This was during the depression, and anyone who can remember that time in Peterhead, will understand the dreadful poverty among the unemployed - many of whom had not worked for years, not because they did not wish to work, but because they could not! There simply was no work for them! Not of any kind!

We kept a supply of clothing and boots in the school. These were given to deserving cases, quietly and unobtrusively. It was not easy because they were so independent!

Mr. Mair was an ideal boss and he gave me a great deal of scope to carry out any idea which was to the benefit of the school, or the children! He even allowed me to purchase football strips and boots!

So many boys were keen on football that we ran two teams in the local schools under fourteen league! The boys were told in no uncertain terms, that football was a game. The idea was plain and simple. The ball had to be kicked or headed between the opponents goalposts. Any kicking or tripping of opponents, no matter what the provocation, would be dealt with - and severely!

I only once had to drop a player for misconduct, and as it so happened, it was one of our "star" players. When the boys showed disappointment at his being dropped I said "He deserves to be dropped - doesn't he?" "Yes Sir - but - "No buts" I said "His worst punishment will be to see you go on and win without him! and you can do it. It's up to you!" They did win and after a few days I had an apology from the boy and a request to get his place back! I told him I accepted his apology but he would have to win his place back! He agreed and I'm glad to say he did win his place once again! Happy, happy days!

Ten past four every school day found thirty to forty boys outside the science room door, eagerly waiting to be taken up to "Barclay" park. There "Watty" Stephen and I would take a side each (usually coaching from the centre-half position). It was quite usual to get home for tea about six or six-thirty p.m. "clarted with dubs!"

One exception to this was Wednesday afternoon. Then Walter took thirty to forty boys to the "baths" from 3 p.m. to 4 p.m. and I followed from 4 p.m. to 5 p.m. with another forty or so. I always stripped upstairs, and always dived in at the deep end off the springboard. There was always an innocent looking bunch of boys standing around the side waiting. Whenever I dived in this group would jump in guessing where I would surface, and they would try to force me under again! I remember that first boy I taught to swim. He was the biggest boy in school. I taught him first to float, and then swimming was simple.

Football - so many names spring to mind! - Mr. Garden, George Beddie (both Central), Alex McBain (Episcopal), Bill Mitchell, Jim Gordon, George Walker (all Academy). These were some of the teachers who gave up so much of their leisure time to teach the young folks not only football but sportsmanship!

Alex McBain was not a teacher but the school "Snappy" (attendance officer). I don't think anyone will grudge me an extra word about Alex! He ran the Episcopal school team - Miss Chisholm was Headmistress there. Alex was so keen on football and young folks that his enthusiasm rubbed off on his young proteges! The Episcopal team might be beaten by 10 or 12 goals to 0 but they were so keen that they turned up again next week for more!

Among the North school boys were Charlie Lawson - when I left the North school he handed me a poem written by his father about our teams! "Pombie" Geddes - one of the biggest hearts in a small body I have ever met, there were two Buchans. One played in goal and the other at centre half. There was Martin at centre forward, fast and deadly both in the air and on the ground, Johnny Strachan, who in later years was to score the goal for Fraserburgh which knocked Dundee out of the Scottish Cup! There were two Sturrock brothers and so many more who are just fast fading memories!

One of the "big Buchans" I used to meet during the summer holidays. He invariably came up behind me on a bicycle in Queen Street, and with a hearty clap round my shoulders would say "well Mr. Nicol, enjoying your holiday!" Martin I have seen only once since school days. I visited a boxing booth on the Embankment one summer evening and lo and behold one of the challengers was my old centre forward Martin. Johnny Strachan I met one day in a shop in Inverurie. We've had several "natters" since about the old days at the North. The old school has fallen on bad times since then. Shifting population, moving out to "Baird's parks" (Hope Street) and Balmoor, has reduced its roll so much that it has now been closed! When I was there its roll was 800+!, memories! - The formation of the Buchan Schoolboys Team, School swimming galas etc!, etc! Happy, Happy Days!

SCHOOLS FOOTBALL IN PETERHEAD IN THE THIRTIES!

In the thirties we had a very good schools football league for the under fourteens. There were two teams from the Academy, Blacks and Whites, two from the North, Greens and Blues, and one from each Episcopal, the Central and Boddam! We had two smaller pitches running across the Academy Senior pitch in Raemoss Park. (The Barclay Park) every Saturday morning I was up there early, lighting the fire to heat the water for the showers (no janitor to do that job for us but only volunteer labour). We found it almost impossible to persuade the boys to take a shower, they would dress and stick their heads under the shower to wet their hair so they they could comb it!

In the North of Scotland schools cup we found that when we were drawn against such teams as Aberdeen schools we were at a great disadvantage. We usually found they had much bigger and stronger boys. The city, of course had a huge pool of players from which to choose, and eventually we decided to amalgamate with, of all people, our "arch enemies" the Brochers! James Gordon, a Fraserburgh Academy teacher (later to become an assistant Director of Education), George Walker (an Academy technical teacher) and myself found ourselves running a Buchan Schools Select, which drew boys from the whole Buchan area! George and I were given the task of scouting for talent and running trials and selecting teams. In the first year we made several discoveries. The best one I think was a boy "Anderson", I think name was. His father was a shepherd, and agreed to leave his boy at school as long as we were still in the cup (Scottish!) We played Aberdeen in the first round of both cups that season, and we beat them each tim! This was mainly due to this lad! He played on the right wing, and I have never seen a better prospect, at his age. I tried to find him after the war, as I was in a position to get him a trial with Aberdeen. I had become quite friendly with the then "Dons" manager.

But, to the game! This laddie, with a long raking stride, with beautiful ball control, a magnificent "double dummy body swerve, and a deadly shot! In the first game, he had a long ball pushed right through in front of him. He picked it up in his stride, and cut into the corner of the penalty box. With a beautiful swerve, he left both the left half and the left back on the wrong foot, and, still on the run, he hit a screamer from the edge of the box. The keeper, running out, flung up his hands, and the ball rebounded between them. Instead of banging the ball, the winger, still on the run, coolly reached forward, and flicked the ball over the keepers head. He knew exactly where the ball was going, and we were one up!

That year Buchan Schoolboys went to the third round of the Scottish cup. In this round we met a team from Fifeshire, I forget which, but from the start it was obvious they had been warned about our winger. In fact they told me afterwards they had been. Soon after the start, Anderson was hacked down and carried off! This was when we made another discovery! Playing one man short, we discovered we had another star! (his ability had been over shadowed by Anderson's brilliance). This was another Mintlaw boy. His name was Parrish (I think his father was a postie). He played a great game at centre forward, but eventually we were beaten. The score was either 2-1 or 3-2, I forget which. I can never forget who was responsible for these two "stars", our old friend Mr. Garden, who had been at Peterhead Central, was now Headmaster at Mintlaw, and although he did not have many boys, he coached and trained them in all that was best in football!

I spent four very happy years at the "North School" and we had our share of laughs among the more serious work of education! Early in the war years we had Glasgow evacuees, pupils and teachers. One Glasgow teacher was an inveterate pipe smoker. Towards the end of each month he was always hard up. We always knew when this was, because he then mixed used tea leaves with his tobacco, and the stench in the staff room was unbelievable! Among the "North" staff in these days were Miss Davidson, Miss Cordiner, Miss (Bessie) Barclay, Miss May Collie (Domestic subjects), Miss Stephen (infants), Miss Milne and Miss Morrison. On the male side we had "Wattie" Stephen who went to Kingswells, and "Cammie" Milne who went to Kennethmont both as headteachers! Miss Davidson became the first Head of the J.I.C. in Wilson Street. She was exceptionally good with the older boys, and taught them to make recorders and play them. She had a recorder and "comb" band in the top class. When she went to J.I.C. I was appointed Deputy Headmaster to Mr. Mair.

THE HUMOUROUS SIDE OF THE HITLER WAR!

I spoke earlier of world war two bombs. Apart from the tragic side there was also, on occasion, the funny side. I was on the St. Mary Street bowling green one afternoon, when the unmistakeable sound by the early Heinkel 111's could be heard. An argument immediately started up "You can tell the difference - you can't!" The argument was soon settled by a new noise - the dreadful whistle of falling bombs! On a seat at the east end of the green sat a figure wrapped in a travelling rug - no names, no pack drill! - but he genuinely had to be helped to that seat regularly, when he came to the green. One moment he sat there wrapped in his rug - an instant later he was up the bank and crouched behind the wall! I can remember a similar occasion when a sudden shock produced an amazing re-action. This was during my Academy days. Next to the tennis courts, opposite the main gate, was a market garden. The owner was pestered by us boys. We were continually kicking balls into his gardens, and when I think of it, we must have often damaged his plants. This day "Bill" Birnie (now Dr. Birnie) kicked our ball in, and so he had to retrieve it! He had just kicked it out, when there was a shout "Here's the mannie!" With a running jump, Bill cleared the fence and reached the pavement! We could scarcely believe our eyes!

About recognising planes by their sound. This was not only possible, but was used regularly! I was declared unfit for military service (I had just came out of a hospital after a long illness) but in Braemar I served as C.O. of the R.O.C. post there, and we were regularly asked "What does it sound like?" Many planes were heard there but not seen because of the hills. We could usually tell, and in time it was routine to identify, among others, Wellingtons, Ansons, Harvards, Hudsons and many more! The early "jerries" bombers were of course unmistakable and they quite often flew down the valley of the Dee at night.

Early in the war, when I was recovering from the illness I mentioned earlier, I was at the North Head with Mr. Sinclair, of Sinclair and Buchan, and a few others. We were standing near the old battery, when a flight of Heinkel 111's (there were seven of them) flew in so low over the water, that we could see, quite distinctly, the crew-men in the perspex noses. They turned over the bay and flew out, passing, it seemed, between the land and Buchan Ness lighthouse. We thought afterwards, they must have been the planes which made an unsuccessful attack on the Forth Bridge!

When the Italians entered the war, an italian ship was scuttled just north of Peterhead. A naval detachment from a minesweeper, salvaged it and refused the pilot's assistance. I was standing on the wall at the north harbour with a group of fishermen, when one of them said, pointing to a piece of broken water, "Jist watch laddie! Yon boatie will run agrun on that reef there, an aifter a day or twa she'll brak her back an disappear!" This is exactly what did happen. The naval skipper was completely ignorant of the tremendous currents around that area, and he lost his prize!

By the way, another humourous side to the bombing (I cannot vouch for the truth of this, but I tell it as it was told to me). The night that several unexploded bombs were dropped in Marischal Street, one elderly gentleman, who was wakened by the "bumps" went down in his pyjamas to see what was what. He thought someone had rapped on his door, but, finding no-one there, he stepped outside and tripped over something. When he scrambled to his feet, he saw he had tripped over an unexploded bomb. Forgetting his dress, or lack of it, he ran! A policeman stopped him running up Kirk Street and said "Come on now, you canna rin aboot in your pyjamas at this time o nicht!" The reply was terse and to the point - "You ging back there an see fit I tripped ower an you'll rin as weel my mannie!"

THE DAY THE BOTTOM FELL OUT OF MY WORLD

Then came the day the bottom fell out of my world, and I thought my teaching days were over. I had been teaching now at North school for nearly three years. My boss Mr. Mair our headmaster, was one of the kindest men I have ever known. He was like a second father to me.

One day he said to me "Are you well enough Peter? I don't like that cough of yours" I had a slight cough, but not anything to worry about. Mr. Mair however was insistent he did not like the sound of it, so eventually I spoke to a friend of mine Dr. George Stephen, who was assistant to Dr. Leith, George laughed and said "You are as healthy as me." I insisted on a thorough examination and he carried this out. Some time later he gave me the dreaded news - I had pulmonary tuberculosis T.B. that dreaded disease. I would have to go into hospital for at least six months, and worse - if a complete cure was not accomplished, I could not return to teaching!

I was nearly a year off work, but - a complete cure was achieved and I was allowed to return to the work I loved - teaching. Mr. Morrison, the then Director of education, visited me personally during my first week in hospital and assured me my job at the "North" was waiting for me. "Your only thought at the moment is to get well" he told me "Don't worry about your job. I'll look after it". Thus assured I could concentrate on getting well again.

One afternoon in February 1939 I was admitted to ward three Woodend Hospital, Aberdeen. After a bath I settled down for the night, Apprehensive? Yes, at home in Peterhead I had left my wife May and my daughter Eva, not yet two years old. My whole future was at stake, and I was determined, no matter what, I would do exactly as I was told, and it certainly would not be my fault if I was not able to return to teaching.

That first night I simply could not get to sleep. The night nurse brought me cup after cup of tea, but they made no difference. I certainly made up for it next day - I slept till well on in the evening.

If I remember rightly there were twenty beds in the ward, and an additional eight or ten out on the balcony. One of the main ingredients in the treatment was fresh air, and we certainly got our share of that. Even on the coldest nights, every window was wide open. A properly made hospital bed meant a gap in front of you and another at your back, down both of which the night breezes blew. The night nurses and I waged a constant battle, with them tucking the sheets in, leaving these gaps, and me pulling them out and tucking them round me - not the mattress. The nurses knew of course, that the eagle eye of Matron making her nightly round, would spot the slightest untidiness in bed.

I soon settled to the daily routine. Six A.M. Wakey, wakey! and a basin of water was deposited next to your bed, and a cup of tea was placed on your locker top. Many a winter morning you woke to find your mug frozen to your locker. After breakfast of porridge, tea and toast, we had a spoonful of that childhood "delicacy" cod liver oil and a spoonful of liquid paraffin. We were weighed regularly. This was the only occasion I was permitted to step out of bed.

After the usual medical examination, X-ray etc. I was told my treatment was to include an artificial Pneumothorax. The ward doctor was an old acquaintance of mine Dr. McBean. His father was the Medical officer for Aberdeenshire schools, and he himself had been a classmate of mine at the University. My introduction to the Pneumothorax treatment was not really as bad as it sounded. A fearsome looking long hollow needle was plunged between two ribs and into the pleural cavity (the space between the lung and its sheath). Sterile air was then pumped into the pleural cavity. The idea was to collapse the infected part of the lung and thus force it to rest. The calcium in the cod-liver oil emulsion and in our diet, would gradually be deposited on the infected part and in any cavity and calcify it. Rather like a dentist filling a cavity in a tooth. The pressure was rather uncomfortable at first, but after a few weeks of "pumping up" it was almost un-noticeable. I well remember a doctor friend of mine, who was doing relief work for our ward doctor, sending for the records to confirm that the pressure for my lung was correct. When he found it was indeed correct, he said "Well better you than me Peter, but here goes" and he plunged the needle in.

The relationship between staff and patients in Woodend was not the normal nurse-patient relationship. We were all long term patients, many alas terminal, and this led to a very homely atmosphere, in ward three at any rate.

In charge was a sister Smith who later saw service in the middle East during the war. Her right hand man (or woman) was Laura the Ward maid. Speak about house proud - that ward was like an advert for Flash, the floor was like a mirror, and Sister Smith would not allow a bed to be moved, not even when lifted, in case it would mark her precious floor. Little did she know that when she went off duty the nurses would lift the beds together so that we could play cards. Two at the foot and two at the head and we were set for our favourite game Bridge. We had a very good Bridge school.

Laura was, beneath her rough, blunt manner, a kindly soul who would willingly go messages for "her" patients, but she completely "blew her top" if she saw a mark on her floor or if she found a sweet paper.

She nearly exploded one Saturday afternoon. A patient called "Dod" Smith regularly got in jokes from Helen Thom's joke shop. This particular Saturday Laura had completed her cleaning for "visiting" hour, and went to tell Sister the ward was ready for inspection. "Dod" slipped out of bed and placed an imitation heap of dog's excreta against the door post. Laura came back, saw this and yelled "Oh my God Sister. A dog's sh - - - on the ward floor" Sister and Laura came rushing in with saw-dust, brush & shovel, and proceeded to clear up. The model of course, gave the show away whenever it "klunked" against the shovel. Give Sister and Laura their due, they laughed as loudly as the rest of us.

Opposite me lay Mr. Cowie from Peterhead. He was a sick man indeed, but probably the cheeriest patient in the ward. He slept very little, and so that we could talk at night, when most of the ward were asleep, he taught me the "dummy finger" alphabet. Unfortunately he died as did the other Peterhead patient a Mr. Strachan.

We had another cheery soul in ward three, a George Greig. George was blind but he was an accomplished pianist. Since he was a walking patient, he regaled us regularly on the ward piano. In the winter evenings we played "Housie" (Bingo). We paid one old penny for a card so that the total winnings amounted to about 1/6 old money (7$\frac{1}{2}$p).

Our daily routine changed on Fridays. This was known as High Cleaning Day. All the beds down one side were lined up in the middle of the floor, and this half of the ward was cleaned and polished until the floor could have been used for a mirror. Then the other side got the same treatment. This routine was rudely interrupted for me one Friday. I was to have my ears syringed. Staff brought a kidney dish, syringe and warm water. She was about to commence when she was summoned to Sister's office. Some twenty or so minutes later she returned, handed me the dish and filled the syringe. She then injected a stream of COLD WATER into my ear. I went out like a light. She had entirely forgotten how long she had been away, and the cold water was as effective as a smack on the chin. She was so apologetic when I came round. That is one High Cleaning Day I'll never forget.

Another memorable time for me was when I suffered a whole week of severe tooth ache. I broke a tooth and none of the Doctors had any experience of extraction. I offered to pay for a dentist to visit. So strict was hospital routine in those days that I was told this was not permitted. The official dentist was due to make his routine visit next week and so I must wait for that. For days on end I had aspirins, bags of hot salt, hot water bottles, you name it, I had it, every conceivable remedy except the one I required - a dentist. I really suffered. When the dentist did arrive - I can picture him yet - he straddled me on the bed and at last the offending molar was out - Sweet relief!

When war clouds loomed nearer, came the day when we were told that every patient who could walk downstairs was to be "evacuated" home. Joy?, Regret? It was difficult to say which came out top. Joy certainly at the prospect of a sudden return home, but a lingering doubt - was this going to spoil the chances of a cure? However on

September 2, 1939 I found myself in a car returning to Peterhead. Next day in Peterhead I listened to Neville Chamberlain's broadcast, declaring war on Germany.

Looking back, I actually enjoyed my stay in hospital, apart from the fact that I was separated from my family and friends. In Ward three Woodend new friends were made.

I spent another two months bed-ridden, and eventually, after a series of "guinea pig" tests I was declared completely cured, and to my great relief I returned to teaching.

All this was in 1939 and today in 1955 I am still hale and hearty and enjoying life to the full. *q*

THE "BARCLAY" PARK AND GOLFING ON CRAIGEWAN!

Back to football, and the "Barclay" park, so called after Mr. Nat. Barclay who was partner in Simpson and Barclay - (now Benzie and Miller) at the top of Broad Street. What a job we had with the "Barclay" park! The fence round it was being continually torn down or cut. There were many unemployed in the "Ives" Park area of the town at this time, and they were not allowed to play football in the School field! This was a challenge! Why should they not be allowed to play there. It was on their doorstep, and most of the time unused! Gates were locked, and so fences were cut or pulled down! There was a telephone at the corner near "Buchan Bowb's" shop and I can picture yet 'Nat" on his bicycle, on his way to Craigewan, he was an ardent golfer. If he saw anyone playing on the school pitches, who had no right there, he would jump off his bike, run to the telephone kiosk, and pretend to telephone the police.

That was usually enough. The crowd would disappear into Raemoss housing scheme, the field would clear like magic, but, immediately Nat's bike disappeared round the corner, along the golf road, the game would recommence!

The other partner in the drapery business, was Mr. Simpson. He was the gentleman we went to if we wished to hire the Recreation Park for a football match or Fete. If he said "No!" it WAS NO, (he usually said "Yes"!) He seemed to have full responsibility for the "Feuars Managers".

I was for many years a keen golfer too. As far back as I can remember the first tee was up on the bank between the old clubhouse and the river, and the first green was along the river beside the creek! At tournament times many of the players used to drive a ball over the river into the field which is now a housing scheme (bungalow's). This is the field which always had a pair of corncrakes every summer. Then the first green became the 18th green on the "New Course". The first tee was now on the bank above, and the first hole was now played up and over the hill! I can remember many incidents at this first hole, but two stand out in my memory. A certain gentleman, who needless to say shall be nameless, was on his way up the hill to play his second shot, when he felt a severe blow in the ball of his leg and he fell in a heap. He looked back at the couple on the first tee and shouted something at them, thinking one of them had driven off too soon. It turned out that a varicose vein in his leg had burst, he had not been shot by a golf ball!! The other incident was one evening when I was playing John Glennie in a competition. I mis-hit my drive into the whins near the top of the hill, but I found my ball lying cocked up nicely. The result was I took my brassie (two wood) and I hit a beauty. We hunted high and low all around the green and at last John said "Only one place left - in the hole". He was right I had holed out in two! I can still see the expression on his face as the threw the ball over to me! I had the good fortune to hole a second shot at the second hole as well - but - this was on another occasion! We spent many happy summers there on the golf course, Tom Beveridge (his father was for many years the club secretary), Charlie and Ben Collie, Tom Gibb, and I. During the summer holidays we practically lived there.

At the short fourth hole there was a field on the left. When it was in corn it was forbidden to enter it to look for your ball. I remember one day one of us hit a ball into the corn, and, determined not to lose it we all went in to look! Fifteen minutes later we were about a dozen balls richer! Most of the seniors tolerated the juniors well enough, but I can recall one rather pompous elderly gentleman who would invariably say "Stand aside you juniors!, I wish to play on!" No names - no pack drill - all I will say is he lived in Landale road, and, he was no golfer! How we laughed when he "duffed" his shot, and under the circumstances he usually did!

Very often we stayed the whole day at Craigewan. Our lunch would be a packet of Abernethy biscuits (three old pence) and a split of lemonade (also three old pennies). Our lunch total was sixpence each (2¹/2 pence). We had a saying "It never rains on Craigewan". I may say it often did and I've had many a soaking to prove it!

THE "BLUE TOON'S" LITTLE SHOPPIES!

Peterhead used to have a great many little shoppies, which were just one room of a ground floor flat, with a counter put in and a shelf on the window sill. There was one at the corner of Back Street and Prince Street (Clark's corner) and another one between the Brethern Hall and Simpsons. Both were served by young lads who had been left alone in the world!

I remember "Patty" Finnie who had one of them. He belonged to "Finny Faul". It was years later that I discovered this was really Whinny Fold a small hamlet South of Cruden Bay. We used to buy "Lucky Tatties" for a "Maik", and if you were lucky inside it you'd find another "Maik" (halfpenny). They were lumps of delicious candy covered in cinnamon! In most you would find a "gee-gaw" of some kind. A cake of chocolate e.g. Cadburys milk or Frys cream cost two old pence. My favourite was Frys Raspberry cream alas no longer on the market. A packet of Woodbines (coffin nails) cost two pence, and a packet of ten players cost six-pence.

Another small shoppie was run by a Mrs. McKeillor in Thistle Street and another at the corner of King Street and Windmill Street. This latter one I had good reason to remember. I cannot recall the name of the elderly lady who ran it but I recall vividly her constant "moan". I delivered her Butteries in the morning, and she was usually in bed. This did not stop her routine - always those wicked bakers who charged her too much for their bread. According to her it was impossible to make a living. We sold to these shops by the "baker's dozen" which meant they paid for twelve and received thirteen. She used to try me to persuade my father to give her preferential treatment! Some hope!

When I finished school I went on to "varsity" but came the day when my future father-in-law Jimmy Macdonald, told me that for all my University training, my education could never be completed until I had seen my fellow men in the "raw" from behind a "pub" counter! - and on a Hogmanay night! I was soon to find out exactly what he meant!

To complete my education - no - that cannot be right, because ones education can never be completed - every day one should be learning some thing otherwise life would become quite meaningless - lets say a completely new angle was being added to my education. My father-in-law I'm sure many "Bluemogganers" will remember Jimmy Macdonald who was for years with the Gas Company. His sister, with her husband Alex Stevenson ran the North Eastern and then bought the Palace Hotel. Every Saturday evening a small hall behind the North Eastern opened from 7 p.m. till 9 p.m. My father -in-law looked after it for Mrs. Stevenson, and he recruited me to assist him.

For a few weeks I looked after the till, and then I was permitted to serve. Behind the bar were Jimmy Macdonald, Bob Whyte, Bill Strachan and me. Out on the floor were several waiters. My eyes were opened that first Saturday to several things. I was introduced to the cellar, to beer in the barrel, and to the broaching and pumping, but my greatest surprise was at the crowds who gathered there to enjoy a pint. One customer in particular I remember well. He was often referred to by the name "white

inch" although he was better known locally as the Peterhead Peter Craigmyle (referee),
I was warned to look out for him. Most people like a froth top to their pint, but this
individual, if there was as much a a skin of froth on his beer would hand it back and
say "I pay for beer not a white inch of froth!"

Saturday nights were busy and eventful - but - oh boy! hogmanay night was there
fun? The back hall was crowded and I think there were seven waiters in the hall, in
addition to the four of us behind the bar. We had our jackets off and our sleeves rolled
up, and the sweat was pouring down our backs. Several trawlers were in the harbour
and when nine o' clock approached, we were prepared for the worst (although little did
I guess what that was to be). Hessian potato sacks were handed over the counter to be
filled with bottles of beer to carry out, and as the ninth hour struck there was still a
queue at the counter 6 to 8 deep. Down came the hatch, and a table was pushed
against the door. We got our feet against it and our backs to the wall, and held the
door shut until the police arrived, and sent the crowd home. No one was hurt - no one
even threatened, but all were determined to get another drink at any price!

When they were dispersed we had time to breathe, and then someone noticed the
floor was spattered with blood. Earlier on I had lifted two bottles from a crate too
quickly, and they had cracked together. One "blew up" and gashed my thumb. We
were so busy that I had simply kicked the bits of glass aside, wrapped a handkerchief
round my thumb and carried on. Bill Strachan had stood on a piece of glass which had
pierced the sole of his shoe and entered his foot. He went off home refusing even to
have it bandaged. I can remember, years later, on a visit to Rora, Bill saying his foot
was itching. He took off his sock and picked out the piece of glass which had been
there all this time!

By the way I forgot what the price of beer was at that time, but I do remember whisky
and other spirits sold at sixpence a nip, and a quart bottle cost 12/6d (62^1/2 pence). I'll
draw a veil over the rest of that hogmanay night, except to say that in the early hours
of New Years day I was mechanically muttering "Happy New Year" and surreptitious-
ly emptying nips of whisky into flower pots!

THE PASSING OF AN ERA, RORA HAS A BLACKSMITH NO MORE!

Bill Strachan, whose name has appeared more than once in my ramblings, has called it a day! Man and boy he served the farmers of the Rora district, working in the "smiddy" with his father, and then taking over after his father died. Many a Sunday when we were visiting, he would be called out to mend a binder or a mower, or a plough, and never did he refuse! For many years he was the only "smith" in the district who would (or could) shoe a horse. I can remember when horses queued at the Rora smiddy waiting to be shod. Latterly not a horse came there. Now the smiddy is sold and a lifetime's collection of machinery and tools had been "rouped" and is scattered far and wide! The smiddy is no longer a place where all the news of the district is brought by the farmers coming to have their repairs done!

The smiddy house really took one into the past - peat fires, girdle scones and oatcakes (breid), creamy milk, fresh from the friendly cow outside the back door, fresh made butter and cheese, and real hens eggs from free range hens, rich and full flavoured. I can recall spending a holiday "ca'in" peats from the moss, driving Bill's father's sheltie to and from the moss, loading and unloading peats and at the same time, filling potato sacks with peat dross. I got "Karun" Baird, who had a coal delivery business, and who was another old school-mate of mine, to take the sacks into Peterhead for me, where I dug the dross into my garden in St. Mary Street. I had a wonderful crop of vegetables that year! The flat we had in St. Mary Street had been occupied previously by Miss Cheyne an old teacher of mine at the Central school, a real lady. The flat under us was occupied by Mr. Robertson (Sandikie) and upstairs was a Mr. Cordiner, a fish salesman, and a Mr. Ritchie, blacksmith at the Drummers Corner. His daughter "Patsy" was married to the late burgh surveyor in Inverurie. Across the road lived the Sangsters. Douglas came to Inverurie as sanitary inspector.

To return to the subject of retirement, I myself retired in June 1975 and many of my old friends are also in retirement - the floors o the forest are a we'ed awa richt enough!

I'll have more time now to sit and think - think of all the things I should have done? - no! rather of all the good times - fun times during student days - indoor bowling with the old fishermen, upstairs in the Masonic Temple and bowling with these same fishermen plus Alan Dalziel and Charlie Cross at the Public green in the summer - etc! , etc!

We had fun times swimming off the end of the embankment, or what is now the Lido or at Sandhaven or Ravenscraig - fun on the links, at Craigewan, in the cobble, in the lifeboat, in the salmon cobbles, emptying the bag-nets (at 4 0' clock in the morning), playing golf, football, cricket - cowboys and indians, pirates you name it, all on the links or the little linkies - making our own kites and flying them - making our own sledges and hoping we would have enough snow to use them - roller skating or playing miniature golf or dancing in the Empress Hall or in the Palace Hotel ballroom - or in the "Muckle Kirk" or the Rescue Hall. I remember the day of the official opening of the Masonic Temple. A fete was held and Jack, Ernest and I went dressed as

"Pip, Squeek and Wilfred of the Daily Mirror cartoon.

Life in Peterhead has turned full circle, or almost. From a Royal Spa in Stuart times it became an oil port in its hay-day of whaling, then a fishing port (herrings), then a holiday resort, and now it has become the most important port in the North Sea oil boom! - after oil what? Who knows? One thing is certain, no matter what lies in the future there will be no return to the terrible times during the depression - post World War One, when real hunger and real poverty were rife in the "Blue Toon", and when many were reduced to scrounging. When ragged children haunted the harbour "scrannin" a fry of herrings, or begging unwanted fish from visitors fishing in the bay, and selling them round the streets. When rickets and T.B. were rife and the St. Peter Street "soup kitchen" was at its busiest, no matter how bad times are forecast for our country, and there are plenty prophets of doom, no matter what, I am sure those days are gone forever. They were there in the first place, only because people were prepared to accept them as "just life!" The present generation just will not accept this!

Let me finish on a more cheerful note. Scottish education these days gets a bit of a thrashing not only by the popular media, but in public! I am convinced that despite all the experiments and innovations - despite the fact that the powers that be were persuaded to introduce many innovations (and not all good ones) from our "cousins" South of the border, Scottish education is better today than ever it was. Where in the old days the "lad o pairts" did well, many, many more not only get the chance but take it! Time and time again I have seen in recent years, pupils who twenty years ago would have been told, "it's no use, you'll never make it!" Being coaxed and encouraged into Higher Leaving Certificate courses followed by College or University. Scottish education can hold its head up high!

Dufton Scott's story of the old Aberdeenshire roadmen is as true today as it was in his day!

A gnarled old roadman breaking stones by the roadside somewhere in Aberdeenshire was talking to an Englishman hiker. The hiker had made it plain he didn't think much of Aberdeenshire.

"So ye widna like tae bide here?" echoed the roadman. "Oh, aye some o's div leave the place. The best o's bide at hame, bit we gae the weaklings a bit o education an, sen, them sooth an they get on a richt there. They get on for managers o' businesses, an doctors, an professors, an stockbrokers. They're a ower England an at the heid o athing!"

Mrs. P. Nicol,   5, 7 & 9 Merchant Street,

31 Prince Street .   PETERHEAD,   December   1936

WORKS: NARROW LANE.

TELEPHONE—PETERHEAD, 136.
ESTABLISHED 1772.

Licensed
Valuators,
Cabinetmakers
and
Upholsterers.

To J. & A. MASSIE.
FOREMOST FOR FURNISHING.

Removal
Contractors
and
General House
Furnishers.

ALSO AT . . . .
85 BROAD STREET, ABERDEEN.

ACCOUNTS RENDERED
QUARTERLY.

1936						
Dec.	17	To 3 P.ce. Chesterfield Suite				
		" Hair Mattress			2	12	6
		" Wire Do		1	2	6
		" Mattress Pad			11	6
		" 4 Sunset Pillows @ /6		1	2	
		" G/Walnut Bedroom Suite		12	15	
		" Do Bed & Rail		2	7	6
		" Occasional Chair		1	8	-
		" 1 Rug			19	11
			£ 31	11	11
		Discount		1	17	11
			£ 35	14	-

25·12·36.

PAID
WITH THANKS

J. & A. Massie
pr.

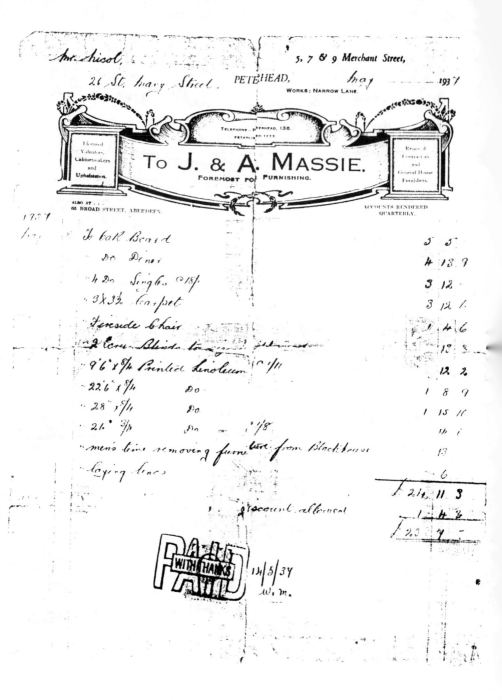

Mr. Nicol,

26 St. Mary Street.

5, 7 & 9 Merchant Street,

PETEHEAD, May 1937

WORKS: NARROW LANE.

TELEPHONE - PETEHEAD, 136.
ESTABLISHED 1773.

To J. & A. MASSIE.

FOREMOST FOR FURNISHING.

Licensed
Valuators,
Cabinetmakers
and
Upholsterers.

Rope &
Contractors
and
General House
Furnishers.

ALSO AT . . .
65 BROAD STREET, ABERDEEN.

ACCOUNTS RENDERED
QUARTERLY.

1937

May

To Oak Board	5	5
Do Dinor	4	13 9
4 Do Singles @ 18/	3 12
3 x 3½ Carpet	3 12 6
Fireside Chair	1 4 6
2 Ecru Blinds to	15 2
9'6" x 3/4 Printed Linoleum @ 7/11	12 2
22'6" x 3/4 Do	1 8 9
28" x 3/11 Do	1 15 10
21" 3/4 Do 7/8	14 6
men's time removing furniture from Blackhouse	13
laying lines	6
	£24 11 3
Discount allowed	1 4 3
	£23 7 -

PAID
WITH THANKS
14/5/37
W. M.